CONSTRUCTING
THE HOLISTIC ACTOR:
FITZMAURICE VOICEWORK®

MICHAEL KEITH MORGAN

ISBN-10: 1466258659

ISBN-13: 9781466258655

TABLE OF CONTENTS

ACKNOWLEDGMENTS

I would like to gratefully acknowledge Catherine Fitzmaurice for her enthusiastic support, availability, and the many blessings her teaching has bestowed. Heart-felt thanks to Saul Kotzubei for his gentle guidance and mentoring. I would also like to extend a deep appreciation to my 2006-certification colleagues, both teachers and students, who will always be my special voice tribe.

I thank Simon Williams, Judith Olauson, and Leo Cabranes-Grant for their encouragement, expert supervision and insights. I would like to recognize the late Robert Egan, who welcomed me to the UCSB community and set a glowing example of scholarship and artistry. In addition, I am very grateful to my BFA acting colleagues for their continued good cheer and cooperation while I played dual roles as teacher and student.

I extend my deep gratitude to Sophia Fox-Long, Harley Shapiro and Margaret Kemp for giving me feedback on early drafts. I would also like to thank Laurien Alexandre, Dean of University-wide Programs at Antioch University, for helping me clarify the organization of the book. I also want to acknowledge Bob Blackford for his invaluable editing skills.

Finally, I want to acknowledge those people who have enriched my life before and during this undertaking. I extend deep appreciation to Margo Sims for introducing me to yoga when I was a teenager, to Florence Winston, my first acting teacher, who kept me focused on high standards in life and art, to Louise Battle, my mother, for her example of tireless, human endurance, and to the memory of my father, Forrest Morgan, whose loving spirit is always there for me.

ABREVIATIONS

ATHE	Association for Theatre in Higher Education
IPA	International Phonetic Alphabet or International Phonetic Association
NLP	Neuro-Linguistic Programming
TCM	Traditional Chinese Medicine
VASTA	Voice and Speech Trainers Association

PREFACE

This research emerged from the need to examine a largely undocumented system of voice training that is gaining popularity in this country and abroad. Currently, in many theater departments around the United States, there is a trend toward globalization, the inclusion of cultural traditions in addition to those from the West. This trend is particularly tangible in the propagation of history and literature seminars on theatrical traditions and innovations from Africa, Asia, and Latin America. There has also been significant impact in the practical arena through including such disciplines as Tai Qi, yoga, Suzuki, and the improvisatory techniques of Augusto Boal in the acting student's curriculum. As a voice teacher and an actor, I was drawn to the eclecticism inherent in Fitzmaurice Voicework, particularly its potential for reaching diverse student populations through blending East/West disciplines. The research was also prompted by the need to understand if such an intercultural foundation provides the actor with more holistic, expressive capacity for a multi-textured, emotionally, intellectually and spiritually enriched voice. While there are a number of extremely effective approaches to voice, and each of these claims to develop a maximally expressive actor, it is the specific contribution of this East/West interchange that concerns this study. Relevant to this discussion is the investigation of how Fitzmaurice Voicework avoids cultural imperialism, while pointing the way to a global approach that invites parity and diversity in methodology.

When I contacted Catherine Fitzmaurice with my idea of writing a theoretical and historical examination of her work, she was immediately supportive and encouraging. To my great advantage, she also insisted that I experience the work deeply and firsthand. I enrolled in a five-day intensive course in Albuquerque, New Mexico in January 2004, which became the prerequisite for my further training as a Fitzmaurice associate teacher. This training involved two intensive months of study in January of 2005 and 2006. Within that year, I also attended private classes with the Fitzmaurice master teacher, Saul Kotzubei, in Los Angeles. Part of the requirement for certification included practice teaching. In the interim between Januaries, I was fortunate to have very enthusiastic student actors to work with through my post as lecturer at UC Santa Barbara. Concurrently, I enrolled in a yoga teacher-training program in Santa Barbara, which was completed in May of 2005. This gave me a better grasp of how yogic theory and practice pertained to the Voicework. Prior to undertaking the dissertation project, I had studied and practiced Traditional Chinese Medicine, which prepared me for a theoretical understanding of the acupressure methods that are incorporated into the Voicework. This research developed, therefore, through a combination of academics and fieldwork. It was significant to my own development to blend intellectual comprehension with experiential execution. While the work itself supports the idea of thinking actors and feeling thinkers, it should be stated that for most students a detailed intellectual acquisition of the theory behind the approach is not necessary for its effectiveness as a liberating system for the voice. This analysis, therefore, is geared more toward those actors or teachers who are familiar with the Voicework. It is not a textbook and does not give procedural details in describing the exercises that comprise the work. In conversation with the originator of the Voicework, Catherine Fitzmaurice, it was decided that a more practical study outlining the exercises would occur in a later publication.

The focus of this present volume is on the unique influences that blended to create Fitzmaurice Voicework. Toward this end, a sequential approach is taken in arranging the material, by examining contributing sources as Fitzmaurice discovered, explored, and included them in the design of her method. Chapter one, the introduction, provides a historical vantage point from which to regard the Voicework's genesis in the context of other major systems of training. While previous research has been done cross-referencing prominent voice systems to one another, this introduction will include Fitzmaurice Voicework, an approach that has heretofore been missing from the discussion. This first chapter also identifies important Fitzmaurice terminology that is pertinent to the comprehension of her work. The second chapter centers on the bioenergetic roots of the Voicework along with its forefather, Reichian therapy. This chapter investigates how the distinction between therapy and art are clarified in Fitzmaurice Voicework. Chapter three scrutinizes the Eastern influences on the work. The main inquiry that guides this chapter is: can an essentially western approach include eastern disciplines in its foundational evolution without losing the need of meeting the demands of western theater and without minimizing those eastern systems that inform it? This chapter includes a detailed discussion of yoga and the Voicework. Through the assessment of subtle body anatomy, including the chakra system, kundalini and tantra, a parallel will be drawn between the super-physical and Fitzmaurice's interrogation of the heightened realm of theater voice. The third chapter will also look at shiatsu and acupressure as forms of somatic therapy that are utilized to further enhance the freeing aspect of the Voicework, known as destructuring. This section of the study examines how the use of therapeutic touch in the actor training setting can be employed as a stress releasing modality without creating dependency on the teacher and without mitigating the necessary dramatic conflict intrinsic to theatrical characterizations. The culminating chapter, the fourth, leads from chaos theory to a metaphoric examination of the principles that undergird Fitzmaurice Voicework. Chaos, in its creative rather than dissipative aspect, acts as a relational frame from which to examine the tension between art and science. This chapter will argue that, through her experimentation, Fitzmaurice is able to bring balance to them in such a way that energizes her theory of voice. While creative chaos has always characterized her experimentations with voice, the connection to chaos theory, came toward the end of the work's evolution, and thus the placement of this chapter is last in the progression. It should be kept in mind, however, that the spirit of creative chaos has always been operating underground in all of Fitzmaurice's explorations and in her philosophical attitude toward liberating the actor's instrument. It is this chaotic element that will give the work its potential durability as it continues to entertain porosity with other growth-oriented systems in the quest of giving the actor more space for vocal unfolding.

In addition to creative chaos, the importance of the breath is a unifying principle that provides a basic pillar for the Voicework. Both themes are ongoing and guide all the theoretical constructs that comprise and invigorate this approach. Overall, the trust of chaos and breath, as creative entrance points for finding one's voice, are the big messages that this book hopes to impart. Chaotic feelings of "fight and flight" when embraced through the agency of breath, rather than braced against, become an unending source of power for the actor's voice.

CHAPTER ONE:
INTRODUCTION

HISTORICAL BACKGROUND

Catherine Fitzmaurice's Voicework has had a significant influence in the area of performance training over the last forty years in the United States and abroad. She started acting at the age of three. When she was ten, she began formal voice, speech and text training with Barbara Bunch, who trained Cicely Berry, the vocal director of the Royal Shakespeare Company. Fitzmaurice's tutelage with Barbara Bunch continued until she was seventeen, at which point she entered the Central School of Speech and Drama in London. Here she studied voice with such prominent teachers as Clifford Turner, who authored <u>Voice and Speech in the Theatre</u>, and Cicely Berry. While at the Central School, she distinguished herself by earning a scholarship and prizes. She later accepted a post there as an instructor of voice, poetry, and text. During her residence in England, David Kozubei, a writer and bookseller, introduced her to the works of Wilhelm Reich and the therapy based on his work called bioenergetics. She studied bioenergetics with Alexander Lowen and began to incorporate this therapeutic system into her Voicework, as a means of helping actors dismantle tension. In 1968 she came to America. In this country she continued her research in bioenergetics and also began to study yoga and shiatsu, all of which would have profound influences on her teaching strategies. Since coming to this country, Fitzmaurice Voicework has been adopted into the curriculum of many important American actor-training institutions. The importance of the Voicework is gaining momentum as Fitzmaurice trains more teachers through her certification course. This study posits that the currency of Fitzmaurice Voicework is rooted in its ability to traverse venues because of its intricate weaving of Eastern and Western theories into a practical discipline that has wide application. The Voicework's evolution will be regarded from an ideological and historical perspective. Actors, singers, public speakers as well as clinicians now utilize the Fitzmaurice system of voice training. This appeal to a diverse population constitutes a restoration and a reconnection between oration, singing, and acting, yet in a thoroughly new orientation.

Early Western history bears out that typically no distinction was made between the preparation of the actor's and the orator's voice. Jacqueline Martin's <u>Voice in the Modern Theatre</u> traces these intertwining roots to the art of rhetoric commencing in the ancient Greek tradition (10). Essentially, actors borrowed from the oratory art in order to fortify the voice through techniques of delivery and style. David Garrick, the celebrated actor of the 1700s, marked a movement away from the declamatory technique that wedded acting to the oratory art with his more 'natural' expression (Martin 8). Cecil Price reminds us, however, in <u>Theatre in the Age of Garrick</u>, that the word 'natural' is a loaded term having special connotations according to the changing vogue of the day (42). It should be noted, moreover, that the art of elocution, an offspring of rhetoric, still held sway both in Europe and in America even into the late 19th century (Martin 9). While shifts were made toward more naturalistic delivery, as noted by Garff Wilson in <u>A History of American Acting</u> (84-7), letters and reviews from that period would indicate that what passed for natural then would not be the equivalent for the term that rose from the theater of realism in the 1950s, which still defines much of the acting style in television and Hollywood films prevalent today.

In America, the history of voice connects with the history of speech. Through a detailed series of articles entitled <u>Standard Speech</u>, that history is explored in the form of a debate between proponents and opponents for a standard. This historical examination notes the influence of William Tilly, an Australian phonetician, who moved to England and later Germany where he trained, among others, the eminent Daniel Jones, who would go on to standardize Received Pronunciation in the still referenced, <u>Everyman's English Pronouncing Dictionary</u>. Tilly immigrated to America in 1918, where he was given a teaching post in the Columbia University extension program, and here he influenced a generation of American speech teachers. Professor Emeritus Dudley Knight, an opponent in the debate and a Fitzmaurice master teacher, argues in <u>Standard Speech</u> that Tilly was the forefather of a prescriptive form of speech called World English Standard, and that his focus on phonetics marked a divergence between the spoken and written word that broke the sway of the Elocutionary Movement (34). Specifically, this shift meant that pronunciation would be based on speaking rather than orthography. While this alteration could lend itself to the use of phonetics as a tool for describing speech sounds, Knight posits that Tilly, and his teachers instead of remaining objective recorders, created a prestige form of American English that was held up as superior to the common vernacular heard in the streets.

Margaret Prendergast McLean, a prominent student of Tilly, with her publication of Good American Speech in 1928, put World English, also called Mid-Atlantic Standard, on the linguistic map. Its proponents considered it a speech form that incorporated phonemes from Standard British and Standard American. These early proponents, such as McLean, regarded it as an upgraded "cultivated" brand of English (Knight 35). Tilly also taught Edith Skinner, whose book Speak with Distinction is still used in drama programs around the country. Mid-Atlantic has lost its supremacy as the standard for broadcasting speech in this country to the Mid-Western based General American. But due largely to Skinner's efforts, Mid-Atlantic can still be heard in many of the great movies of the 1940's and by actors trained in that style – especially in classical plays such as those authored by the ancient Greek dramatists, Shakespeare, Ibsen, and Chekhov. General American, noted by Knight as a misnomer for Inland Northern (Standard 77), became a rival standard to Mid-Atlantic with the publication of A Pronouncing Dictionary of American English in 1944, although the author, John Kenyon, warned against a favored brand of speech. The ongoing and unfinished debate is beyond the scope of this study, and the reader is referred to the Standard Speech, mentioned above, for arguments for and against an American standard, but its relevance to Fitzmaurice Voicework will be noted below.

The history of voice training also intimately connects to that of acting training in America. James McTeague's Before Stanislavsky: American Professional Acting Schools and Acting Theory, 1875-1925 presents an in-depth study of early establishments in this country. In 1871 Steele MacKaye opened the Saint James Theatre and School in New York City. In examining the voice program created for this first institution of formal acting instruction in America, the influence of Francois Delsarte is clear, "In stating the purpose of the institution, MacKaye claimed to be 'the only living pupil in this country' who had studied with Francois Delsarte, and indicated that the Frenchman's teachings were to be followed" (McTeague 17). Delsarte's method was a complex system of oratory based on a trinity of language, thought, and gesture with a religious underpinning evoking the Father, Son, and the Holy Ghost. This mystical design points to the loftiness of this system, in which language was considered the least important of the three, and gesture the most important agent of this triad for effective communication (Cole and Chinoy 188). The Delsarte system is quite detailed in its theory with a decidedly spiritual base underscoring a power below the word, which is divine. The subject of spirituality reoccurs in the discussion of Fitzmaurice Voicework, as it does in the late theories of Wilhelm Reich, a major influence on her approach. Regardless of this association, it will be clarified through the discussion that while there may be some affinity between Fitzmaurice Voicework and Eastern spiritual concepts, she does not predicate a system built on theological foundation as Delsarte did.

Another school discussed by McTeague is the New York School of Acting, later renamed The American Academy of Dramatic Art in 1892, where again in the spirit of Delsarte, pantomime and movement were elevated in importance over voice (65-6), and elocution was *de rigueur* (85). In Boston, the Emerson College of Oratory was opened in 1880. The significance of this school's philosophy was that it subordinated the actor to the author, the interpretation of literature being its highest aim (McTeague 96-7). Also in Boston, Leland Powers opened the School of the Spoken Word, emphasizing intellect over emotion in 1904 (McTeague 162). Margaret Prendergast McLean was the Head of English Diction and Edith Warman Skinner was an acting student at this school. Both would go on to have significant influence in the area of speech training in America as noted above. All of the schools examined by McTeague had a moral basis (14-5), often connected to religion, which manifested in the ear-centered correctness of speech and delivery. This legacy was continued with the importation of Stanislavski by way of Richard Boleslavsky, a former member of the Moscow Art Theatre, who came to America in 1922. He opened a school in New York, the American Laboratory Theatre and employed Margaret Prendergast McLean as the voice teacher, thus assuring the dominance of Mid-Atlantic as the preferred way of speaking English on the American stage.

Singing, too, had its own methods, and with no clearly distinct vocal regimen, the actor often partook of the rigors of musical techniques in order to develop speaking ability. Michel Saint-Denis, who was instrumental in shaping the curriculum of such major training institutions as The London Theatre Studio, The Old Vic Theatre Centre, L'Ecole Superieure d'Art Dramatique, The National Theatre School of Canada, the Julliard School Drama Division and The Stratford Studio of The Royal Shakespeare Company (which were all established between 1935 and 1962) recommended voice training for the actor based on singing. Saint-Denis does qualify this, however: "We are not speaking here of beauty or musicality for their own sake; our concern is to awaken in the actor a musical and poetic sensitivity capable of being translated to the stage by the rhythmic quality of the voice and by modulated tones conditioned by the text. All this must start from within and find its full outer expression through the voice" (110). This qualification, however, did not stop some actors of that generation from "singing" the text. Constantin Stanislavsky is considered the alternative forefather to Saint-Denis for establishing a modern actor training technology. In Building a Character, Stanislavsky's orientation to the speaking voice is also based on singing: "The principal result of my work, however, was that in speech I acquired the same unbroken line of sound as I had evolved in singing and without which there can be no true art of the word" (102). With Stanislavsky, there must be acknowledged also a decidedly mystical underpinning, akin to Delsarte in the study of voice: "Do you not sense that particles of you are carried out on these vocal waves? These are not empty vowels; they have a spiritual content (Building 84)". This "spiritual content" will be carried forth into the current work of Catherine Fitzmaurice. The spiritual theme, while secondary to the practical applications of theater, links Fitzmaurice with pioneers as Delsarte and Stanislavsky in a holistic agenda that extends to a wide variety of voice professionals. In bridging the speech/singing gap, for example, a Fitzmaurice master teacher, Joan Melton explores this connection in her book, One Voice. Melton notes in her Introduction:

> The work of Catherine Fitzmaurice figures prominently in the overall perspective and approach to voice training in this book. Fitzmaurice Voicework or Destructuring/Restructuring, effectively integrates voice and movement, has a solid physiological base, and facilities a healthy and beneficial dialogue between the theatre voice training and the training of singers for a variety of media. It is also an invaluable tool for the retraining and healing of virtually any voice that has been misused or abused (xii).

Melton identifies a number of factors in common between training for the spoken and sung word that form the argument for a unified system of study, while also clarifying the specific needs and requirements of the individual art forms. For example, distinct from one of the pitfalls of oratory, neither Melton nor Fitzmaurice advocate singing the text. The focus of the present study will lean decidedly toward the application for the actor while acknowledging a potential common ground, both in theory and practice, of the Voicework for singing.

CURRENT STATE OF THE ART

As Delsarte's principles calcified into a rigid system of rules and as speech training alienated many actors who perceived it as elitist, prescriptive and prejudicial, a rift developed between those proponents of elocutionary techniques and representational acting. With the rise of Realism in the American theater starting with the formation of The Group Theatre in 1931 and the flourishing of The Method in the 1950s, the actor was encouraged to turn away from what many perceived as the artificiality of the Mid-Atlantic Standard. As Nan Withers-Wilson notes in Vocal Direction for Theatre: "The Group Theatre's commitment to the production of indigenous American plays by Americans and about Americans meant that most of the characters portrayed did not speak in a Standard American or Transatlantic dialect" (10). But with that rejection and the dismissal of oratory methods, a void was left in the training scene with regard to voice and particularly with respect to the classics. The first publication of Arthur Lessac's book, The Use and Training of the Human Voice in 1960 restored interest in voice training, although his method was firmly rooted in musical elements borrowed from singing and a unique adaptation of the International Phonetic Alphabet. Nonetheless, Lessac advocates a synthesis that resonates with the integrative work of Fitzmaurice when he states:

> In its broader sense, 'speech' usually includes ...aspects of vocal expression, such as intonation, inflection, accent, emphasis, nuance, modulation – everything used to convey intellectual content as well as emotional impact. Singing, in the broader sense, should be the same thing except that the vowels sounds are sustained longer than in speech...Cleary, all the vocal arts and all the speech skills form a single discipline. To compartmentalize this discipline into polarized fields would be as counterproductive as training the left and right hands of a pianist separately. The discipline resists compartmentalization because vocal life does not, indeed cannot, exist apart from physical and emotional life" (Use 10).

Nevertheless, in spite of a potentially inclusive philosophy, in application Lessac's approach and Fitzmaurice Voicework are very distinct. An important contributing factor to this distinction is Fitzmaurice's emphasis on the breath through destructuring and her specific mobilization of the transversus muscle in the phase of her work called restructuring.

Bonnie Raphael in her article "A Consumer's Guide to Voice and Speech Training" points out that Lessac, unlike many of his contemporaries, attempts to pull away from the authority of British based systems and teachers of voice training by creating a uniquely American approach (209). Raphael's article has a Neuro Linguistic Programming orientation from which she assesses four major approaches: Traditional, Skinner, Linklater and Lessac, in light of auditory, kinesthetic or visual emphasis. These sensory modes are related to how people think as described in Richard Bandler and John Grinder's book, Frogs into Princes. Since there is an overlap of these three means of information gathering, Raphael doesn't diminish the systems she discusses to a single sensory modality. Nonetheless, the NLP method of classification helps to give some distinction of one system from another. For example, Kristin Linklater's work is distinguished from Skinner's by Linklater's kinesthetic rather than auditory emphasis (Raphael 208). A rival system to both Skinner and Lessac emerged with the innovative work of Iris Warren, which Kristin Linklater brought from the UK to America in the early 1960s. With this importation, the actor began to claim a voice system apart from oration, standard speech and singing. Linklater's use of this groundbreaking approach moved toward giving the actor a discrete methodology of training; it also created a separation between singers, public speaker and actors. Therefore, this recent development in the history of voice training, while focusing on and empowering the actor, also set up clear demarcations insisted on by its practitioners. With the work of Fitzmaurice, the separation is potentially healed in the sense that her work has appeal to all three groups.

Any theoretical discussion of the work of the great voice and speech teachers is of necessity reductive. All of these master teachers will claim a physical, emotional and intellectual synthesis, although the emphasis and the entrance points may shift. These extraordinary teachers are always best in the complexity of their own voices. However, in order to give a context to the Fitzmaurice approach that will be the focus of this study, it is necessary to acknowledge the fertile field in which she works and give a brief summation that attempts to capture something of the unique flavor of these pioneering instructors. I will undertake this in the following literature review that directs the reader to the sources. There are a number of textbooks by the major voice and speech teachers, Clifford Turner, Cicely Berry, Arthur Lessac, Kristin Linklater and Patsy Rodenburg. This is not an exhaustive list of remarkable teachers but it is intended to limit the discussion to those eminent educators that in the recent past, approximately the last fifty years, or currently occupy that part of the field in most proximal relationship to Fitzmaurice. In addition to their considerable influence through published works, this selection is also justified by the importance of their coaching of many well-known actors and their training of numerous teachers to populate the field.

Berry and Linklater's books are written in pairs, with the first book dealing with relaxation, breathing and vocal production and the second dealing with text. Berry's Voice and the Actor and The Actor and the Text are handbooks growing out of her experiences with private coaching, the Central School and the RSC. Cicely Berry's commitment of privileging the text is evidenced when she writes:

> The vocal transformation of yourself into another character must come from the words and rhythm of the writing; if this leads you into a different way of speaking that is fine, provided no tension comes from it. The words and thought must lead you to a way of speaking and if you start by thinking of finding a different voice or of putting on some sort of sound which is distortion of your own voice, it will limit you and be a strain and most probably will lack simplicity (Voice 132).

In this statement, Berry seems to be rejecting the oratory precedent of the 'voice beautiful' with a decided shift from the singing model to a speaking one. This distinction is clarified when she further states:

> It is important to recognize the difference between training the voice for singing and training it for acting, because many misconceptions can arise about where sound should be placed. For both you need to open up everything you have, but for singing you convey your meanings through the particular disciplines of sound – the sound is the message – so that the energy is in the resonance. For the actor, on the other hand, the voice is an extension of himself and the possibilities are as complex as the actor himself, and so it means a basic difference in the balance of sound and word. For the actor, ultimately it is the word that must impinge, as it is the word which contains the result of his feeling and his thought; it is therefore in the word that his energy must lie, and in the million ways of

stressing, lengthening and inflecting it. This is why an overbalance of head tone does not communicate to an audience – it does not reinforce the word (Voice 16).

Fitzmaurice would agree with this overview, but, while attending to the specific communicative needs of the actor in regard to the spoken word, her work goes deep into that aspect of training characterized by Berry as opening up "everything you have". It is in the depth of this formative, exploratory work in the areas of her method that she calls destructuring and structuring that Fitzmaurice offers a foundation that supports both singers and actors. Once this basis is provided, the training can proceed in a specific vocal direction depending upon the textual or musical demand.

Berry's emphasis on "making the language organic, so that the words act as the spur to the sound, and so that flexibility and range are found because the words require them" (11) continues in her manual The Actor and the Text. Relevant to this study, Berry's physical rooting of words would support the need for the foundation of an innovative usage of body arrangements known as tremor positions that are primary to the Fitzmaurice Voicework. Berry provides an important prompt for Fitzmaurice Voicework's psychophysical evolution when she writes:

> Just as breathing is a vital function, so the need to make sound to
> convey our needs is vital. Words came about because of the physi-
> cal needs to express a situation. Think for a moment of expressions
> like 'my heart came into my mouth', 'my hair stood on end', or 'my
> hackles rose' – there are atavistic phrases which tell you something
> of your response to fear and of being attacked. You have these sen-
> sations when you are frightened and certain anatomical changes
> take place (Voice 17).

In this statement, Berry catches the essence of the "fight/flight" syndrome that will become a theoretical cornerstone in the Fitzmaurice Voicework discussed in this study. The network of exercises developed from this theory will give Fitzmaurice Voicework its unique flavor.

While a critical assessment of Berry's work may suggest that it could lead an actor to an over reliance on the written word, Kristin Linklater's approach provides an entrance through the body and breath that postpones the actual speaking of text until a much later point in the actor's development. In <u>Voice in the Modern Theatre</u>, Jacqueline Martin distinguishes the work of these two teachers:

> To sum up, Cicely Berry's approach to the vocal delivery of a classical text is principally through the text itself, whereby the actor is encouraged to involve himself actively in the structure of the thought at the moment of communication. Once having this security of meaning, he should then be able to determine how his voice and sound can best convey this thought. Only by following this line and by avoiding a heavy emotional involvement will he have a chance of sharing the structure of the text with the audience. Conversely, Kristin Linklater's approach is based on the organic functioning of the voice, which, when liberated, receives its impulses from the senses and consequently informs the text (178).

While both teachers desire an organic outcome with language rooted in an anatomical, emotional and intellectual being, generally, one may describe Berry leading from the outside and Linklater from the inside. Fitzmaurice seeks a balance and leads from both the interior or psychophysical entrance point as well as from the formality of textual analysis.

Linklater's <u>Freeing the Natural Voice</u> had a powerful impact in American voice training. She makes an essential modification of awareness by advocating sensing the voice rather than listening to it:

> An unremitting effort will be made, in this and subsequent chapters, to shift the job of judging sound from the aural to the tactile sense. As long as work on the voice includes listening to sounds to check their quality, there will be a conditioned split between the head and the heart, and emotion will be censored by intellect rather than shaped by it. By the 'touch' of sound, I mean the feeling of vibrations in the body, and initially that sound will be explored as another inhabitant of that central part of the body already housing breath, feelings and impulses (35).

In her book on text, <u>Freeing Shakespeare's Voice,</u> Linklater continues to take a visceral approach to language:

> Many actors have been trained to experience vowels only in their
> mouths and ears – for them also the emotional content will be miss-
> ing. But anyone who can relax the stomach muscles and allow the
> breath to drop deep down into the belly, and then drop the thought
> of a vowel down after the breath, will immediately understand that
> vowels are the emotional component of words. Emotion and appe-
> tite and creative impulse are inextricably connected in the central
> nervous system (15).

It is important to understand, however, that Linklater does not reduce the complexity of intricate text to mere emotional connection. She also adheres to a
vigorous mental functioning, especially when grappling with the vastness of
Shakespeare: "Speaking Shakespeare demands a balance of emotion and intellect to the highest degree. This equipoise is achieved little by little, first by balancing emotion and intellect in the formation of the words, then in combining
them to formulate the emotional and intellectual story of the text" (Shakespeare's
Voice 15). Thus, unlike the early schools of oratory, Linklater does not privilege
intellect over emotion. Instead, emotional connection both precedes and informs
intellect and is never subjugated by it. She is diametrically opposed to the Powers
School of the Spoken Word, which exalted intellect over raw emotional impulse,
and is theoretically at odds with both McLean and Skinner who were affiliated
with it.

Patsy Rodenburg was Cicely Berry's student at the Central School. Currently,
she is the vocal director at the National Theatre in London. She has also taught
very extensively at prominent schools in England and internationally. Rodenburg
distinguishes herself from her predecessors through resurrecting the word
'technique':

> I am going to advance the notion that voice work can often be most
> effective if we learn to work from the outside in. By that I mean
> working from the purely physical and systematic aspects of our-
> selves (the outside) towards the emotional and intellectual life (the
> inside). Over the past twenty-five years most vocal training (and
> most books on the subject) has stressed quite the opposite approach:
> working from the inside out" (Right 113-4).

She may, in fact, be referring to Linklater who states, "The kind of teaching that we focused on at the ATHE conference and to which I clearly belong is the inside-out approach to training the actor" ("Thoughts" 6).

Rodenburg's first book, The Right to Speak is universal in its introductory statement, and she distinguishes this book by making it user friendly to all speakers and less exclusively to actors, as the title bears out. Her second book, The Need for Words, while concluding with theatrical texts for practice, still recognizes how cultural, political, social and gender issues influence a wider public that is not limited to but inclusive of actors. One of the outgrowths of her broadening of the readership leads to a questioning of the sanctity of the Received Pronunciation Standard. Rodenburg regards RP as a standard among other standards (Words 76) that an actor chooses in accordance to the demands of the part. Artistic choice to utilize this standard does not justify its authoritative sway as a class weapon of superiority (Words 79). Following this logic, she sees phonetics as a tool to be employed in the learning of speech sounds without a "robotic" adherence devoid of emotional liveliness (Right 244-5). On the other hand, Cicely Berry, as former vocal director of the RSC, doesn't confront the political, cultural and social stresses around the standard issue but does identify a shift in her awareness pertinent to her work strategy:

> When I began work with the Company, it was geared to 'voice production': this meant training the voice to be clear and interesting, and the speech to be articulated 'correctly' – i.e., acceptable to upper-class standards. But, as I worked more and more closely on the productions themselves, I became deeply aware of the physical connections between the making of the word and the emotional motive of the actor – in the terms of Stanislavski, the want/need of the character in the scene ("Secret" 25).

Rodenburg's invitation to a transparent connection between characters and styles of speaking, may, therefore, finds its roots in Berry, her predecessor and teacher.

Kristin Linklater, in Freeing the Natural Voice, condemns all standards as "arbitrary" (Shakespeare's Voice 13) and futile. This is also stated earlier in Freeing the Natural Voice:

> Such standards last longer between the covers of a book than on the tongues of living people and are a lost cause because live communication will not sit still and behave. Much of what, in the past,

was hopefully labeled Standard American, Transatlantic Speech or Standard English, was a reflection of class consciousness and as an attempted aesthetic rule of thumb is doomed to failure. Yesterday's beauty becomes today's camp and today's ugliness may pass for tomorrow's ultimate truth (144-5).

Linklater also eschews the International Phonetic Alphabet, seeing it as an "over-used" science imposed on the art of acting that robs language of its innate sensual nature (Shakespeare's Voice 13). Instead, she proposes an expansion and a freeing of the actor that gives permission to alterations in speech according to content and context without drilling in prescribed sounds. However, later she would go on to endorse the nonprescriptive speech work of Louis Colaianni when he introduced a more tactile approach to the IPA via his "phonetic pillows" with the publication of his book, The Joy of Phonetics and Accents. Continuing the standards discussion, Lessac also rejects the idea of an authoritative standard. Like Rodenburg, he ascribes to the notion of the actor's choice (Human Voice 251-2). But while rejecting a standard based on education, class or popularity, he does prescribe a "Universal Standard" based on intelligibility, clarity of articulation and a code of personal conduct (Human Voice 253). Fitzmaurice maintains a relationship with the International Phonetic Association (IPA) as a member and she is essentially of the same mind as Dudley Knight, who holds that the actor's acquisition of speech sounds works best in a non-judgmental, non-prescriptive environment. Her work explores ways of making this acquisition visceral by maintaining the sensory experience of the sounds in the mouth while also exercising the ear in maintaining accuracy. With speech, she suggests an expansive, inclusive approach in developing all of the sensory apparatus of the actor, including finding the life of the sound in the body via movement. Standards, dialects and accents are learned in the spirit of increasing the mouth and ear's capabilities, while extending the imagination with a focus on keeping the breath rooted in the body in an ongoing process of creating character structure organically.

Clifford Turner's Voice and Speech in the Theatre contains both voice and text components in one volume. Turner's book was originally published in 1950 and was, therefore, the first of the lot under discussion. Of significance to this study is the fact that Turner taught Fitzmaurice at the Central School. In addition to adhering to the prescribed standard of the day, RP, he also included the controversial Rib Reserve exercise, a method connected to singing, where breath is retained in order to sustain the voice to the end of the sentence or several phrases:

> Thus, with the hands in position, a full breath is taken. Breath is then exhaled by raising the diaphragm, but when this has taken place the ribs are not allowed to descend but remain extended. The diaphragm is then contracted to replenish the breath supply, and again is allowed to rise to expel a quantity of breath. Breath is alternately inhaled and exhaled by the diaphragm which contracts and relaxes rhythmically (17).

Fitzmaurice no longer uses this technique, though she does use his rib swing mobilization that allows a gradual releasing of the ribs in direct relationship with the stream of breath/sound needed to fulfill communication.

PSYCHOPHYSICAL TECHNIQUES

The most recent approaches to voice are often called psychophysical techniques. Mary Corrigan in her article, "Psycho-Physical Techniques and Their Relevance to Voice and Actor Training", broaches questions that are particularly timely in the current training scene where ancient Eastern and contemporary Western healing and spiritual practices interface with traditional voice training. Involving body and mind, psychophysical techniques are holistic, that is they view the actor from the vantage of somatic, mental, emotional and spiritual integration. Therefore, while employing exercises involving isolated awareness, the thrust of the work is essentially moving the actor toward synthesis with multiple entrance points. The hologram becomes a metaphor for this kind of work where the whole is contained in a part. Such strategies for the actor tend to be inclusive rather than exclusive, although ultimately artistic choice making and clarity of a defining action must grow out of this multiple path exploration. Holism allows for a more permeable body of work, and thus Alexander, Feldenkrais, Yoga, and Bioenergetics, to name a few somatic disciplines, are readily absorbed and influence the basic voice methodology. Before centering on the psychophysical alchemy of Fitzmaurice Voicework that occupies the bulk of this study, it is important to acknowledge that her work is part of a larger trend in actor training. For example Lessac asserts:

Actor training, when truly integrated, (1) involves the optimal exploration of human skills and talents, be they physical, emotional, artistic, intellectual, intuitive; and (2) provides a creative problem-solving resource for such related areas as an energy-systems approach to body ecology, crosscultural education, physical training, body-voice-speech therapy, and research in identifying body synergies, among other areas ("Body Wisdom" 3).

Linklater frankly traces the psychophysical roots of her work to F. Matthias Alexander and Iris Warren (Natural Voice 2-3). While Rodenburg warns against the inappropriateness of the overt practice of psychological probing in a voice class (Right 17), she does recognize a therapeutic side-effect when she states, "I would never claim that voice work is psychologically therapeutic (that's one of the dangers to be avoided), but as a kind of physiotherapy it does release hidden memories encased in the body. To that extent it is exceedingly therapeutic" (Right 64-5).

By coming under the psychophysical rubric, all these approaches have potential for therapeutic outcomes. They all look to recover an essence that is linked to vocal vitality. Cicely Berry identifies this as "a private recognition" ("Secret Voice" 29), while Lessac hopes to assist the actor to "rediscover and regain much of the instinctive body wisdom that we lost along the way and then some" ("Body Wisdom" 15). Linklater fully embraces the curative implications of the undertaking when she notes:

> In fact, we are training the person who will become the actor and therefore we are inevitably inhabitants of therapeutic territory because we are restoring a lost sense of illimitability. It does not seem such a bad thing really; if we believe that one of the missions of theatre is healing we can accept the fact that healing goes on in the microcosms of theatre we call classrooms ("Thoughts" 6-7).

Consistently, Rodenburg finds that:

> Each discovery takes us deeper into ourselves. Layer after layer of our lost vocal potential is revealed. Sensations are unknown and yet strangely known until, one day, the realization that we have found our own voices, not the ones that we have been forced to use, but our lost ones. And it is always a voice that is compelling to the

listener because the barriers are down, the mud and grime of all those years of fear and judgment washed away. It is now what it has always been, but dug up and cleaned ("Lost Voices" 38-9).

Through this recovery work, all of these master teachers are tapping into creativity, for it is through the unearthing process that the actor is poised to make choices about new voices, new modes of behavior when the energy released is wedded to text. Ironically, the new is birthed from the matrix of the old.

This study looks at the unique psychophysical synthesis of bioenergetics, yoga, and shiatsu with traditional voice training observing how these interfaces develop into the system known as Fitzmaurice Voicework. I will argue that the Fitzmaurice approach is the most highly evolved in its synthesis of Eastern and Western influences and that this unique transaction of disciplines creates a holistic harmony that provides potential for reaching a varied student population. Synthesis is at the very core of the work, from its proposal to heal the mind/body split through efficiently reconnecting the autonomic nervous system with the central nervous system, to the harmonizing of diaphragmatic action with intercostal and transversus muscle coordination; from inner seeing reflective of meditation in motion, known as tremoring, to a focus-line involving the awareness of incorporating the outer world. The importance of this work in relation to developments in the American actor-training scene has to do with the rise of psychophysical techniques. As Corrigan points out more systems such as Tai Chi, Aikido, Suzuki, Qi Gong and Yoga are included in the curriculum of acting schools. Corrigan notes that often these ancient and esoteric methods are introduced in ways that could pose problems for the acting/voice student if offered out of context by teachers who have insufficient training in these practices (103). She also suggests the important foregrounding of art over therapy that Fitzmaurice would agree with: "Students enroll in a course for voice or actor training, not necessarily for better mental health or interpersonal functioning. If the latter should occur as a by-product, all to the good, but it is not the basis of voice or actor training" (104). No matter how profoundly therapeutic Fitzmaurice Voicework is, the originator of this approach keeps a firm handle on its practical applications in the theater. Further, Fitzmaurice would agree with Corrigan's inquiries relevant to the ethics of teaching, "Let us always ask ourselves: 'Why am I using this exercise? How does it relate to enhancing the skill and proficiency of this class of students? Do I have sufficient expertise to responsibly teach these techniques? Will it help them as actors'" (105).

Because of her in-depth background in pluralistic trainings, Catherine Fitzmaurice is eminently poised to achieve a successful track record of elegantly merging these various disciplines through a lifetime of study and instruction. As such, she is at the vanguard of an elite cadre of voice teachers who bring expertise from various fields to support the actor's expressiveness.

The history of voice and speech in America has been marked by heated controversy. Dudley Knight's article on standards and the pointed rebuttals it evoked bear witness to this fact. It is not within the scope of this study to settle this debate nor will this examination draw a judgmental comparison between so called rival approaches to voice training for the actor. Bonnie Raphel's "different doors into the same room" (212) philosophy is probably an instinctively cherished view held by most actors who want to maintain a wide palette for creative endeavors. I believe that this philosophy can be applied to research in the arts as well. It is important in classifying voice and speech approaches to not calcify their possibility for growth and evolution. Each system is complex and alters its meaning depending on the individual interface between the actor and the work. There is also the potential for the occurrence of a discrepancy between the intention of a system's originator and the application by its followers. This is an ongoing matter of pedagogical concern relevant to all of the approaches discussed in this study. It is in the experimental laboratories of the classroom, prior to naming of 'technique', the gravitational pull of rival camps, the crystallization of exercises, that the actor can recover and unearth limitless possibilities for vocal expression. Just as the actor must make the transition from the studio to the stage, another challenging bridge occurs for the researcher committing the lively practice of voice training to the page. In the open-minded spirit of the Fitzmaurice Voicework, this examination will undertake a charting of its theoretical and historical evolutionary course, while acknowledging, like the language that the voice expresses, that it is a vital entity subject to growth and change.

BASIC FITZMAURICE TERMINOLOGY

This section will serve as a reference for descriptive terms that will occur in the study. To render these definitions free from the author's interpretation, they will be offered as direct quotes from Fitzmaurice:

> **Destructuring:** The Destructuring work consists of a deep exploration into the autonomic nervous system functions: the spontaneous,

organic impulses which every actor aspires to incorporate into the acting process. The tendency of the body to vibrate involuntarily as a healing response to a perceived stimulus in the autonomic 'fight or flight' mode (as in shivering with cold or fear, trembling with grief, anger, fatigue, or excitement) is replicated by applying induced tremor initially through hyper-extension of the body's *extremities only*, thus leaving the *torso muscles* free to respond with a heightened breathing pattern. At the same time a great deal of unaccustomed energy, waves of tremor, and, ultimately, relaxation, flow throughout the body, sensitizing it to vibration, and increasing feeling and awareness. The introduction of sound into these positions allows the ensuing physical freedom to be reflected in the voice too, not just the body, because this freedom also naturally affects resonance and laryngeal use, so that pitch range and inflectional melody are improved, as are tone, timing, and rhythm, and even listening and interrelating ("Breathing is Meaning" 248-9).

Fluffy Sound: My own adaptation for voice work of bioenergetic tremors and yoga stretches exists in their combinations and in a focus on a fully relaxed torso to allow maximum spontaneous breathing movement, and more specifically, *in the use of sound on every outbreath, no matter how the body is breathing, without changing the placement or rhythm of that breathing.* This accustoms the actor to the integration of breath impulse and tone, while it tends to use only semi- approximated vocal folds resulting in 'fluffy,' released, feeling sounds which are very soothing to overused, tense vocal folds, and which can resemble the sounds that, according to Charles Darwin (1969), precede language, and which give individual paralinguistic meaning to speech ("Breathing is Meaning" 250).

Structured Inhalation: The 'structured' inhalation in intentional breathing for speaking is activated by the Central Nervous System (CNS) and is primarily stimulated by ideas formed in the mind, so that the regular rhythm of respiration is altered to express the complex rhythms of thought. (The word 'inspiration' denotes both mental and physical activity.) There is generally a quick intake in preparation for a sustained outflow which vibrates the somewhat approximated vocal folds. In this inhalation the CNS effects the active contraction of the external intercostals, lifting and widening the ribcage, which pulls the now mostly passive diaphragm wider and down, thus expanding the lungs. The seventh through twelfth ribs, where the lungs are largest, are the most flexible, because they are not attached in front to the sternum but only jointed at the spine, so this intentional inhalation focuses effort at the center of the tuxedo cutaway-like portion, but the entire ribcage may be somewhat involved ("Structured Breathing" 3).

Structured Exhalation: The 'structured' exhalation for speaking follows the quick structured inhalation almost instantly. The CNS effects an active quick contraction (and resulting inwards movement) of the transversus abdominis only, which holds this contraction steady throughout vocalization. Because of the accompanying relaxation and rise of the diaphragm the abdominal wall will move further inwards during phonation, but the initial action moves inwards immediately as far as it comfortably can. (I use the image of a trapdoor, hinged at the end of the sternum, drawing inwards and upwards to create a floor for the thorax – the same action as when one tries to appear skinny if standing sideways and looking in a mirror.) One can see at the same time, in a whiplash effect, a passive continued outward movement of the ribs, if the inner intercostals and/or other abdominal muscles are not unnecessarily bracing them in place or starting a contraction to squeeze the ribcage inwards. The outer layer of the abdominal wall (the rectus abdominis) and the middle layer (the obliques) remain uncontracted, soft, and passive, but of course, as an integral part of the abdominal wall, they move inwards together with the innermost layer, the transversus. As the vocal folds adduct and partially engage and vibrate, the external intercostals 'float' down slowly, in a delayed release, not a collapse, and not a squeeze. But the focus is on the action of the transverse ("Structured Breathing" 3-4).

Restructuring: Then, after carefully integrating the unconscious (autonomic nervous system) patterns with the conscious (central nervous system) pattern of rib swing/abdominal support, speech sounds and then speech are introduced as an extension and application of the primary breathing function of oxygenation. This is what I call Restructuring. Restructuring gives the actor control over the timing and the variety of delivery choices of pitch, rate, volume, and tone, and allows approximate repeatability without loss of either spontaneity or connection to impulse.

Restructuring, then, is not only the introduction of intercostals and abdominal breath management into the act of speaking, but is also the harmonizing of that pattern with the individual's physical and/or emotional needs for oxygen moment to moment. It requires the ability to isolate particular parts of the abdominal muscle and of the intercostals and back muscles, without interrupting the organic oxygen need. The Restructuring work for the inbreath expands the chest cavity where the lungs are the largest, in the lower third of the ribcage, thus bringing in as much air as needed phrase by phrase without undue effort in the upper chest but also without inhibiting any movement that might occur there as a result of physical need or emotional involvement. I do not teach Clifford Turner's 'rib-reserve,' but the actor will find that as the body accustoms itself to the Restructuring the ribs will naturally stay out somewhat longer during speech because the abdominal support movement (as the Restructuring work for the outbreath) becomes the vocal action, replacing the rib-squeeze or neck tension which often seem to recur when the actor only attempts to stay 'relaxed' while speaking. Speaking requires an active use of the outbreath during its role as excitor of vibration ("Breathing is Meaning" 250-1).

Focus-Line: The 'focus line' (as a mental image only) then extends from the dynamic action at the abdomen down and around the pelvis and up the spine into the head and out of the 'third eye', so the attention is not on oneself, nor on the vocal tract, but on the point(s) of communication ("Structured Breathing" p.4).

The following study is devised into three sections. The next chapter will look at the origins of the Voicework in regard to Reichian therapy and bioenergetics, and the third will discuss the theoretical ground for intersection and deviation with the Asian disciplines of yoga and shiatsu. The final chapter will be a metaphorical examination of Fitzmaurice Voicework and chaos theory.

CHAPTER TWO:
INTERSECTIONS WEST

INTRODUCTION

Fitzmaurice Voicework is permeable and intersects with three main subjects: bioenergetics, yoga, and shiatsu. In this chapter and the next, I will discuss how these three studies inter-relate through their convergences and distinctions with each other as well as how they inform the Voicework. The intention is to present an interdisciplinary framework that will yield insights into the foundation and development of the Voicework's theory. Chronologically, bioenergetics was the initial thread that wove the formation of this system of voice training, followed by yoga and shiatsu. Therefore, the sequencing of the discussion will be predicated on this arrangement. The bridges between the subjects, however, ultimately create a web of synergistic scaffolding mirroring the mutual contributions of the three foundational pillars. It should be kept in mind that preceding the influence from these areas, Fitzmaurice was already immersed in the traditional application of theater voice training through her studies at the Central School in London. Since there are a number of books examining this kind of practice and theory, especially those by Cicely Berry and Clifford Turner, the focus of my discussion will regard the influences that create the unique flavor of the Fitzmaurice approach.

In 1956, Alexander Lowen and John Pierrakos, students of Wilhelm Reich, the prominent psycho therapist who viewed sexual health as the basis of curing neurosis, developed the system know as bioenergetics. This system codifies Reichian principles into dynamic physical postures. Lowen designed Bioenergetic Analysis in conjunction with Pierrakos as:

> ...a therapeutic technique to help a person get back together with his body. This emphasis on the body includes sexuality, which is one of its basic functions. But it also includes the even more basic functions of breathing, moving, feeling and self-expression. A person who doesn't breathe deeply reduces the life of his body. If he doesn't move freely, he restricts the life of his body. If he doesn't feel

fully, he narrows the life of his body. And if his self-expression is constricted, he limits the life of his body (Bioenergetics 43).

One of the primary goals of bioenergetics, therefore, is to restore the natural multi-dimensional motility to the body. Lowen states that "Body motility is the basis of all spontaneity, which is the essential ingredient of both pleasure and creativity" (Pleasure 48). Both Voicework and bioenergetics aim to salvage the involuntary movements from the consciously controlled manipulations that have been imposed upon them. In the Voicework, this particularly extends to the removal of muscular inhibitions that constrict sound production. These techniques are so rooted in the work of Wilhelm Reich that it is essential to examine his theories to understand the "bioenergetic revolution" and its subsequent influence on Fitzmaurice Voicework.

REICH VERSUS FREUD

In 1965, Catherine Fitzmaurice, newly graduated from the Central School met with David Kozubei, a writer and book dealer, who introduced her to the works of Wilhelm Reich. Reich trained under Sigmund Freud but later moved away from Freudian psychoanalysis and developed his own method to assist clients to mental health. Reich proposed a radical alternative with the method called "character-analytic vegetotherapy" that he developed to recover orgastic potency:

> Its basic principle is the re-establishment of biopsychic motility through the dissolution of character and muscular rigidifications ("armorings"). This technique of treating neuroses was experimentally substantiated by the discovery of the biolelectric nature of sexuality and anxiety. Sexuality and anxiety are functions of the living organism operating in opposite directions: pleasurable expansion and anxious contraction.

> The orgasm formula which directs sex-economic research is as follows: Mechanical Tension → Bioelectric Charge → Bioelectric Discharge → Mechanical Relaxation. It proved to be the formula of living functioning as such (Function 8-9).

In looking at the Voicework, this dense statement and formula must be deconstructed.

From the onset, it is important to determine the grounds for Reich's ideological dissent, since his reactions to Freudian analysis would later indirectly inform the Voicework theory. Reich's criticism of Freudian analysis was based on the argument that mere consciousness of psychological problems through Freud's talking cure was not sufficient in itself:

> If the analyst allows the patient to speak at random, he finds that the patient tends to *circumvent* his afflictions, i.e., to conceal them in one way or another. If the analyst wants to arrive at a correct appraisal of his patient, he must begin by asking the patient *not* to speak. This measure proves very fruitful, for as soon as the patient ceases to speak, the emotional expressions of his body are brought into much sharper focus…

> *human language also often functions as a defense.* The spoken word conceals the expressive language of the biological core. In many cases, the function of speech has deteriorated to such a degree that the words express nothing whatever and merely represent a continuous, hollow activity on the part of the musculature of the neck and organs of speech. On the basis of repeated experience, it is my opinion that in many psychoanalyses which have gone on for years the treatment has become stuck in this pathological use of language (<u>Character</u> 360-1).

This deferral of "human language" will figure into the justification for Fitzmaurice's use of "fluffy sound" as a prelude to the re-introduction of speech. Fitzmaurice defines "fluffy sound" as continuous sound that reflects breathing impulses through a relaxed torso. She claims that because "fluffy sound" occurs through partially closed vocal folds, the effect is "soothing" to strained voices ("Breathing is Meaning" 250). Fluffy sound becomes a vehicle for giving expression to the tremoring, destructuring terrain of the body. It is meant to reveal rather than conceal the inner core of the organism.

Distancing himself from Freud, Reich found that the preoccupation with the ego and the superego was inadequate to bring a person to non-neurotic behavior. As an alternative, Reich held that a fully functional healthy being needed to establish a vital somatic connection (<u>Function</u>151). Instead of a schism between mind and body, Reich proposed a construct based on their unity: "...the physiological behavior determines the psychic behavior, and vice versa. The fact that the two mutually influence one another, however, is far less important for the comprehension of the psychophysical relation than everything which supports the view of their functional identity" (<u>Character</u> 351). In this way, Reich virtually merged mind with body in a fluid equation that would provide an essential premise to the Voicework.

Additionally, Reich rejected Freud because he saw his position as pessimistic. Frustrated with finding cures for intractable cases, and unable to reconcile the tension between inner drives and social injunctions–Freud attributed to humanity a death instinct contrapuntally poised against the libido. Putting confidence in the intrinsic restorative capacity of nature, Reich, on the other hand, took a perspective that was essentially optimistic. This division reflected in their stance on art, for while Freud saw art in terms of neurotic fantasy made acceptable through sublimation, Reich professed a healthy view of the artist in sync with natural impulse: "No great poet or writer, no great thinker or artist has ever escaped from this deep and ultimate awareness of being somehow and somewhere rooted in nature at large" (<u>Cosmic</u> 280). In Fitzmaurice Voicework this natural context is viewed as an empowering matrix from which the actor draws.

Further, Reich saw in Freudian therapy collusion with the social structure that kept people in a state of disease through the imposition of restrictive judgments on sexuality when he wrote, " Psychoanalysis became an abstract and then a conservative 'theory of cultural adjustment,' with many insoluble contradictions.

The conclusion was irrefutable: *man's longing for life and pleasure cannot be checked, whereas the social chaos of sexuality can be eliminated*"(Reich's italics) (<u>Function</u> 219). Therefore, social structure could disrupt and transplant the natural biological structure inherent in humanity's essential being, generating an alternative kind of "social chaos" (<u>Function</u> 226) masquerading under the guise of order. The "social chaos of sexuality" from Reich's viewpoint was at root actually a healthy longing for satisfying natural, instinctive drives. These drives became chaotic when restrained and repressed by social injunctions forcing them underground to manifest in various neurotic behaviors. The "social chaos of sexuality" in this sense equates with confusion. Reich held that ultimately Freud's psychoanalysis inadvertently endorsed this confusion by wanting people to conform to the established moral constructions of society. Reich, it will be seen, had his own morality, but it was based on an inherent trust of the biological structuring forces within nature and he sought to break down the artificial social constructs that were imposed upon that deep inner energizing core. These Reichian theories provide the terminology for Fitzmaurice's destructuring and restructuring work, as well as prompt her to seek to offset induced repressions manifesting as vocal inhibitions with the play of creative chaos as opposed to social chaos.

THERAPY OR ART?

The integration of Reichian principles into voice training opens up the rich dialogue between therapy and art since Reich's thesis and goal as a healer are essentially therapeutic, and Fitzmaurice's orientation as a performance teacher is primarily artistic. While permeability is possible, the overall trajectory of the Voicework must be clearly held in focus, which is a maximally expressive actor. The aim of this study is to understand how Fitzmaurice reframes therapeutic technology in order to render it viable for the actor training to deepen and expand creative potential. In spite of its essential artistic priority, it must be acknowledged, however, that Fitzmaurice Voicework is a psychophysical method, as are other systems that require the actor to encounter various facets of self, mind, body, and emotion. The pedagogical goals overlap with bioenergetics in offering exercises through which:

> ...the person begins to sense how he inhibits or blocks the flow of excitation in his body; how he has limited his breathing, restricted his movements and reduced his self-expression; in other words, how he has decreased his aliveness. The analytic part of the therapy helps him understand the *why* of these mostly unconscious inhibitions and blocks in terms of his childhood experiences. He is helped and encouraged to accept and express the suppressed feelings in the controlled setting of the therapeutic situation (Lowen, The Way 9).

Generally, Fitzmaurice Voicework does not focus on the analytical aspect of discovery, *the why,* though it doesn't avoid such information. Instead, more emphasis is placed on a visceral understanding of how inhibiting blocks appear in the body and what to do to release them. Though methods may vary, most trainers of actors would agree that the quality of aliveness–"one capable of fully experiencing the pleasures and pains, the joys and sorrows of life" (Lowen, The Way 9)–is an asset for performers in theatrical mediums. Lowen challenges the idea that neurosis is a prerequisite for talent when he writes: "A healthy individual has no limitation, and his energy is not bound in muscular armoring. All his energy is, therefore, available for sexual pleasure or any other creative expression" (The Way 15). Yet, Fitzmaurice makes clear distinctions for the classroom when she states:

> Both art and therapy posit perhaps a place of authenticity, a centre point, elements of transformation, and in my terms, energetic geometry and harmonics. However, in destructuring, I am not looking to do psychoanalysis, a judgment attitude in a way, but rather to allow free rein towards "chaos" and self-regulation... Yes, there's overlap, however, and many people have spoken of the therapeutic effects of destructuring/restructuring, but my original intention was for economy of physical effort and improved physical functioning, mainly of the breathing, but also, as a great by-product, of the larynx and vocal dynamics such as pitch, rate, volume and the resonance factor (E-mail to the author. 27 Sept. 2005).

Reich provides a justification for a linkage that cohabits very easily with Fitzmaurice's intention:

> When a man takes pleasure in his work, we call his relationship to it "libidinous." Since *work* and *sexuality* (in both the strict and broad senses of the word) are intimately interwoven, man's relationship to work is also a question of the sex-economy of masses of people. The hygiene of the work process is dependent upon the way masses of people use and gratify their biologic energy. *Work and sexuality derive from the same biologic energy* (Mass 293).

While this is not a study on the complexity of psychoanalytical terminology, it is important to define both "sex-economy" and sublimation, as they are relevant to creativity, including the Voicework. By "sex-economy", Reich is proposing the innate regulation of sexual longing and activity that is only possible in a healthy uninhibited individual. It implies a strong sense of self-possession and propriety that grows out of respect for natural impulses rather than codes dictated by society. Instead of inducing feelings of shame and guilt built on rejection, this proposition suggests nurturing and trusting the child's biologic needs at each stage of development. Further, Reich did not discard the Freudian process of sublimation as a means to express sexual energy in socially acceptable forms. But he held that Freud's idea of sublimation was misunderstood by its equation with sexual frustration and repression of the libido. Reich clarified that sublimation at its best occurred as an expressive rather than a repressive function (Character 187). In order to sublimate an urge or impulse it had to be free, while rejection of that impulse precludes any kind of choice toward sublimation since the impulse remains pushed down. Reich equated the competence of sublimating through endeavor with the ability to achieve orgastic potency. Otherwise, work was abused compulsively as a form of repression and denial of sexuality. Not only did he regard this behavior as undermining the biologic instincts but also as compromising the quality of the work done since the self was divided into laboring action and repressive reaction to the compelling subterranean sexual urges (Character 188). It is important to ascertain how Fitzmaurice Voicework grows from this premise while keeping a clear perspective about the application.

In Fitzmaurice Voicework, sexual energy infuses vocal expression through sublimation from impulses freed during destructuring. The Voicework, however, is not the equivalent to Reichian therapy in that it does not inquire into the bedroom activities of the students, and in fact, Reich's work is often misinterpreted as being limited to such activities. The linkage is more general and ideological and can be appreciated when Reich writes:

> Orgasm anxiety constitutes the core of the universal, biologically anchored pleasure anxiety. It is usually expressed as a general anxiety about every form of vegetative sensation and excitation, or the perception of such excitations and sensations. The pleasure of living and the pleasure of the orgasm are identical. Extreme orgasm anxiety forms the basis of the general fear of life (Function 161-2).

If performance anxiety or stage fright derive from the same source as orgasm anxiety, then Reich's ideological structure provides an efficient under-girding to the Voicework in assisting the actor to retrieve pleasure, often by re-membering those tendencies that emerged in childhood and led both to the desire to act and to play. "Orgasm anxiety", in this scenario, serves as a template for the suppression of instinctive needs and drives. The Voicework attempts to liberate these drives by returning the actor's perceptions to heightened sensation and excitation in order to endow creative impulses with more vitality. In The Function of the Orgasm, Reich asserts: "The severity of every form of psychic illness is directly related to the severity of the genital disturbance. The prospects of cure and the success of the cure are directly dependent upon the possibility of establishing the capacity for full genital gratification" (96). This is too literal for Fitzmaurice Voicework. Here "genital gratification" is read as creative capacity and fulfillment.   While Reich goes into an elaborate distinction between a neurotic and genital character (Character 328), Fitzmaurice simplifies the terminology for application to her work when she clarifies: "Neurotic = blocked; Genital = Free in Fitzmaurice Voicework terms…Looking out at eye level, making the world your peer, taking in what is out there, listening, assisting – these are all aspects of 'genital' behaviors which we teach, which hopefully do carry beyond the theatrical arena" (E-mail to the author. 27 Sept. 2005). Lowen's perspective reinforces Fitzmaurice's, providing more foundational substratum to the Voicework:

> The unresolved emotional conflicts of childhood are structured in the body by chronic muscular tensions that enslave the individual by limiting his motility and capacity for feeling. These tensions, which grip the body – mold it, split it, and distort it – must be eliminated before one can achieve inner freedom. Without this inner freedom it is illusory to believe that one can think, feel, act, and love freely (Betrayal 127).

The fear of play, antithetical to creative stage work, configures with anxiety and blockage of impulse: "Anxiety, as the basic direction opposed to that of sexuality, coincides with the process of dying" (Reich, Function 378). As previously noted, Reich rejected Freud's death instinct, that innate tendency toward self-destruction juxtaposed to life preserving urges, "There is no biological striving for unpleasure; hence, there is no death instinct" (Character 225). In this, his prognosis for humanity was essentially optimistic. Fitzmaurice takes a similarly positive perspective and extends it to consider anxiety as a fertile start point for transformation. For her, creative death for the actor is often the womb for rebirth. To the extent that anxiety offers the possibility for freedom and growth as tensions are destructured into flowing energy, it constitutes an opportunity. In this regard, the term *breakthrough*, often applied in the Voicework setting, evolves from Reich's discussion of masochism that he characterizes as a conflicting mechanism, "The desire to burst is counteracted by a deep fear of bursting" (Function 254). This conflict manifests in patterns of muscular holding. The body, therefore, becomes the gateway to the desires that are housed within it. A breakthrough involves the mobilization of the body from holding pattern to flowing energy with a shift in perception that yields insight. It is this moment of relearning, embraced in the Voicework that finds its roots in Reich:

> In a short time, I had a profusion of facts at my disposal. They reduced themselves to a concise formulation: *sexual life energy can be bound by chronic muscular tensions. Anger and anxiety can also be blocked by muscular tensions.* From now on, I found that whenever I dissolved a muscular tension, one of the three basic biological excitations of the body, anxiety, hate, or sexual excitation, broke through. I had, of course, succeeded in doing this before through the loosening of purely characterological inhibitions and attitudes. But now the breakthroughs of vegetative energy were more complete, more forceful, experienced more affectively, and occurred more rapidly. In the process, the characterological inhibitions were loosened spontaneously (Function 270).

The significance here is the relationship occurring between a mind/body conceptualization that provides a tangible basis of procedure for Fitzmaurice Voicework as well.

This concept lifts psychoanalytical ideology from the spatial limitations of the traditional chair/couch configuration of the therapist's office and offers a potential empowerment through movement and tactile possibilities. Reich initiated this innovation by making awareness of physical constrictions palpable to his patients through actual physical contact, and Lowen brought the psychophysical process to further fruition through activation of the body as noted by the bioenergetic therapist, John Conger:

> Reich worked with people lying down; with Lowen, the vocabulary of man's movement expanded to the potentiality of the dancer. If in fact the body and mind are two sides of the same coin, the unrestricted movement of the body represents a dramatic release from psychological restriction and death. As a therapist, to work with the body lying down is more useful in the context of a full range of postures, including standing, reaching, stretching, bending, and hitting. Reich had developed the concepts of holding back, collapse,

surrender, and the orgasm reflex. Lowen developed in the standing posture the concept of grounding, in which the standing body needs to feel the function and strength of the legs, supporting itself in the world. Lowen's postures developed a more flexible ego, able to integrate the regressive outpourings of the prone position. Lowen was also able to find useful postures in Eastern disciplines and also use the Eastern concept of centering in the *hara* (belly) (184).

In the Voicework, the student is no longer assigned a place but can begin to explore the freedom of a voice that is not restricted either in time or space. Through her experimentation, Fitzmaurice questioned the semi-circular arrangement of students placed around the teacher at the Central School in London. There is also an inference here to the relationship between placement in the class with placement of the voice, since prior methods for training actors taking authority from singing designed techniques that looked for well-placed, pear shaped tones. Rather than adhering to these prescriptions for sounding and sitting, Fitzmaurice sought to give the actor wider parameters. In the Voicework, the actor breaks through time and space. This occurs via mental transits from present to past memories, by inhabiting new zones of physicality in destructuring, and from gleaning information to create new modes of sounding in restructuring. As a wider and denser field of play emerges in the physical body, the voice is informed and one's past habits are interrogated to empower the actor toward both present and future self-transformation. Freedom of voice is linked to the body's own motility, and since character holding patterns manifest in unique ways, the student is invited to explore a terrain that is individual in the recovery of sound. The alignment with Reichian theory allows the dynamics of the sexual act to serve as a template in such exploration because of its association with the life force–its connection to primal energy and metaphorically drawing from sexual coupling–for its potential of holistic union between the diverse parts of the psyche and body.

The two phases of the sexual act that Reich identifies, the flow to the genitals "characterized essentially by the sensory experience of pleasure" and flow away from the genitals toward the full body "characterized by the motor experience of pleasure" (Function 108), relate to the involvement of both branches of the autonomic nervous system–the sympathetic and parasympathetic–that provide a practical and theoretical ground plan for the Voicework. It is the arousal of the autonomic nervous system that connects the actor with the instinctive self and gives vocal expression its authenticity. "Involuntary bioenergetic convulsion of the organism and the complete resolution of the excitation are the most important characteristics of orgastic potency" (Function 108). Reich's "convulsion" translates into Fitzmaurice's "tremor". Fitzmaurice Voicework bases the actor's creative urges in the same primal, biological terrain. It is the permission within action that characterizes this potency and that interfaces power with vulnerability. The ability to let go under pressure, pleasurable or not, is the exercise elicited through tremoring and speaks to the actor's psyche both in the rigors of the art and the vicissitudes of the profession. This is why Reich repudiated that ejaculation was the same as orgastic potency. Surrender, not conquest was the key factor that distinguished his sexual theory:

> The more precisely my patients described their behavior and expe-
> riences in the sexual act, the more firm I became in my clinically
> substantiated conviction that *all patients, without exception, are*
> *severely disturbed in their genital function.* Most disturbed of all
> were those men who liked to boast and make a big show of their
> masculinity, men who possessed or conquered as many women as
> possible, who could "do it" again and again in one night. It became
> quite clear that, though they were erectively very potent, such men
> experienced no or very little pleasure at the moment of ejacula-
> tion, or they experienced the exact opposite, disgust and unplea-
> sure...He merely wants to prove his potency or to be admired for
> his erective endurance. This "potency" can be easily undermined
> by uncovering its motives. Severe disturbances of erection and
> ejaculation are concealed in it. In none of these cases is there the
> slightest trace of involuntary behavior of loss of conscious activity
> in the act (Function 100).

In Fitzmaurice Voicework, it is this involuntary behavior balanced with conscious choice that enhances the creative work. The goal is familiar and referenced in many systems of artistic training that prescribe an ability to unleash potent energy whether imaginative, emotive, somatic, or sexual, and harness, marry, or ride it with some kind of conscious technique. What is particular to the Voicework are the pregnant references that develop out of Reichian therapy and help construct its ontological basis. Ejecting sexual energy, for example, finds theoretical harmony with projecting the voice.

Fitzmaurice faced with the projective demands made on the actor's voice in the theater with the often inherent pushing and straining that went with such demands found an antidote in Reich's concept of surrender:

> Erective and ejaculative potency are merely indispensable precon-
> ditions for orgastic potency. Orgastic potency is the capacity to sur-
> render to the flow of biological energy, free from any inhibitions;
> the capacity to discharge completely the dammed-up sexual excita-
> tion through involuntary, pleasurable convulsions of the body. Not
> a single neurotic is orgastically potent, and the character structures
> of the overwhelming majority of men and women are neurotic"
> (Function 102).

The ideological seeds of Fitzmaurice Voicework are here in such keywords as 'sur-render', 'flow', and 'pleasurable convulsions'. The surrender to flow becomes the aim of tremoring, and orgastic energy infuses the sexual act as it does the tremoring voice. Tremoring is intended to summon forth the resources of the autonomic ner-vous system; to strengthen the connection to both sympathetic and parasympathetic branches.

Following his thesis, Reich divides sympathetic and parasympathetic operations under anxiety and pleasure syndromes respectively (Function 290). In a rudimen-tary way sympathetic activity can be seen as contractive and parasympathetic as expansive but these branches work in a harmonized fashion and formulate a gestalt of coordination. Both action and reaction ensure the survival of the organism, and arousal, as well as synergistic flow, completes the functional unity of the organism. Most directly for voice work this unity is seen in the breath. Reich gives a descrip-tion of respiration in terms of sympathetic and parasympathetic functioning, "This enables us to comprehend the life process, respiration in particular, as a condition of continuous oscillation, in which the organism is continually alternating between parasympathetic expansion (exhalation) and sympathetic contraction (inhalation)" (Function 295). In Fitzmaurice Voicework, the capacity to surrender is intrinsic to restructuring where intercostals and transverses muscles engage and let go in tan-dem. This capacity for surrendering is also approached through allowing the tremor to flow through the body, and the medium for that flow is the breath. When the breath encounters the rigidity of muscular holding in a semi-stressful bioenergetic position, survival instincts are elicited that serve as a source of information about both physical and mental processes. By heightening awareness of these 'fight/flight' mechanisms, Fitzmaurice Voicework moves toward recovery of primal aspects of creativity that empower ratiocination. The underpinning to Reich is both ideological and practical in his description of this survival mechanism:

> First of all, it had to be understood that the process of muscular tension in sexual excitation could not be the same as the process of muscular tension in anxiety...In sexual excitation, the musculature is contracted, i.e., prepared for motor action, for further contraction and relaxation. In an expectation fraught with anxiety, on the other hand, the musculature is gripped in a *continual tension* until it is released by some form of motor activity. Then either it gives way to paralysis if the fright reaction takes place, or it is replaced by a reaction to motor flight. The musculature can, however, remain tense, i.e., not resolve itself in either of the two forms. In this event, that condition sets in which, in contrast to *fright paralysis*, can be designated as *fright rigidity* ("scarred stiff"). Observation shows that, in fright paralysis, musculature becomes flaccid, is exhausted by excitement; the vasomotor system, on the other hand, reaches a state of full excitation: acute palpitations, profuse perspiration, pallidness. In the case of fright rigidity, the peripheral musculature is rigid, the sensation of anxiety is missing or is only partially developed; one is "apparently calm." In reality, one cannot move and is as incapable of physical flight as of vegetative escape into the self (Character 343-4).

ARMORING

Chronic fear incarnate in Reichian terms is called 'armoring'. Reich discusses this concept at great length in Character Analysis, where he writes: "We are of course familiar with the transformation of infantile demands and anxieties into character traits. A special case of this kind of transformation is the replacement of a phobia by a definite kind of armoring against the outer world and against anxiety, an armoring dictated by the structure of the instinct" (198). Destructuring is the apt term used by Fitzmaurice to dissolve, via tremoring, the body armor that limits access to the actor's inner resources for creativity. Armoring is not a required part of the human condition. If one follows Darwin's theory, with the evolution of man to an upright position, the vulnerable exposure of the soft ventral parts don't dictate the necessity for armoring, since, unlike animals that move about on all fours, humans have the freedom of the arms and hands for defense. In line with this argument, Elsworth Baker, a Reichian therapist, makes an important distinction between two types of armoring:

> Armoring may be divided into natural or temporary muscular contraction and permanent or chronic contraction. The former occurs in any living animal when it is threatened, but is given up when the threat is no longer present. The latter originates in the same manner, but because of the continued threats is maintained and becomes chronic, reacting eventually to permanent inner rather than environmental dangers. In this discussion armoring refers to the latter type (29).

Referring to Reich's "orgasm formula" clarifies that all tension is not problematic. This is relevant to the Voicework in its goal of helping the actor distinguish positive life-affirming tension needed to support creative impulses from the kind of tension that locks such impulses in a rigid body. Reich identified a number of armored character-types that formed specific character structures such as hysterical, compulsive, phallic-narcissistic, masochistic, and schizophrenic. Structuring in and of itself is a natural part of character formation. It provides a person with identity. Armoring is a special kind of character structuring that suggests a pathologically restrictive tendency, although it should be noted that the terms are sometimes used interchangeably in the literature outlining Reichian theories. Reich, however, does make a clarification by classifying "character" according to its reactions to external influences that cause a habitual pattern. This is juxtaposed to those traits and abilities that are native and don't constitute armoring:

> By character, in short we mean an essentially dynamically determined factor manifest in a person's characteristic demeanor: walk, facial expression, stance, manner of speech, and other modes of behavior. This character of the ego is molded from elements of the outer world, from prohibitions, instinctual inhibitions, and the most varied forms of identifications. Thus, the material elements of

the character armor have their origins in the outer world, in society (Character 171).

In addition to this clarification and the one given earlier by Baker between temporary and chronic tension, Lowen also distinguishes between character and character structure. His definitive distinction is that character is a healthy, conscious choice, whereas, character structure is pathological and largely unconscious (Bioenergetics 338).

In her approach, Fitzmaurice distinguishes character armor from character, as did Lowen. In Fitzmaurice Voicework, identity emerges from the moment of exploration and can alter with a new moment or insight as the actor exercises the ability to flow and commit to the stream of sensations, images, thoughts and feelings that are awakened in destructuring. "The feeling of identity is based on the awareness of desire, the recognition of need, and the perception of body sensation" (Lowen, Betrayal 232). While an ever-changing continuum of flowing sensations suggests a constantly shifting sense of self, the repetition of the journey in the Voicework also increases a personal awareness of one's ability to make choices that reinforce and characterize one's unique process of becoming. In this experience, one begins to distinguish character choice from crystallized structures that originally occurred as subconscious armoring reactions. Thus, inflexible character structuring is replaced in the Voicework through a process of destructuring and restructuring by fluid shaping according to natural needs and the desire to communicate them.

In Bioenergetics, Lowen provides a description that also applies in the Voicework, "Armoring refers to the total pattern of chronic muscular tensions in the body. They are defined as an armor because they serve to protect an individual against painful and threatening emotional experiences. They shield him from dangerous impulses within his own personality as well as from attacks by others" (13). Armoring, therefore, prevents flow from both the interior and the outside, and as such it shuts down communication. In the Voicework, the tremor is employed to dislodge the locked energy via subtle and large movements of the armored structure. In such a process, it assists the body in unleashing the array of past tensions that it contains:

> In the conflict between instinct and morals, ego, and outer world, the organism is forced to *armor* itself against the instinct as well as against the outer world. This armoring of the organism results inevitably in a limitation of the total ability to live. The majority of

people suffer from this rigid armoring; there is a wall between them and life. This armor is the chief reason for the loneliness of so many people in the midst of collective living (Reich, Sexual 4).

In tremoring, these chronic tensions and the stories they tell resonate through a speaking body. They can then be further integrated into the actor's craft by supporting communication. Armoring prevents the actor from full, living potential as contradictory forces wage battle in the body. Tremoring permits the actor to give voice to these conflicts, not in the psychoanalytical method of verbal discourse but in the pre-verbal vocalizing of the tremor in the phenomenon known as "fluffy sound".

TREMORING

It is chronic fright rigidity that is addressed in Fitzmaurice Voicework through tremoring. The apparent calm or placid mask of social etiquette serves as an entrance to awaken the old instinctive urges that are buried beneath it. To this end, in Fitzmaurice Voicework it is important to distinguish tremor from spasm. Chronic muscular spasm operates to hold the body in a state of denial from the experience of flow. In this state, biologic energy and muscular tension develop an adversarial relationship as the tension attempts to suppress the energy that becomes rebellious. This interface between suppression and rebellion becomes the spasm. From this perspective, the body can be viewed as a battlefield of conflicting impulses and directives. The tremor, as employed by Fitzmaurice, is conceived as a means of deconstructing tensions and bringing the body into harmonious flow. Reich supports this suppressive aspect of spasm: "In the pelvis, as everywhere else in the province of the living organism, inhibited pleasure is transformed into *rage*, and inhibited rage is transformed into *muscular spasms*" (Character 389). Tremoring, on the other hand, converts the process of holding into one of release. Fitzmaurice offers a clarification when she states:

> I believe Reich meant spasm as a condition of locked muscle tissue, which can be lifelong, longish, short, or something which one feels as a painful knot and a bump, which can release after a few days – a cramp that won. Tremor is unimpeded flow of energy and wave and shimmy. The lay use of the word spasm, or even "spaz" could refer to a resisting of flow, or the experience of a lightning-like shudder.

> Perhaps, it's the body trying to tremor, but the person doesn't allow
> it (E-mail to the author. 27 Sept. 2005).

The rebellious impulses are given free reign as one moves from spasm to tremor, and in the shift, an unconscious terrain becomes palpable where the autonomic responses kick in. Below the tension is a substratum of fear since that emotion is so interwoven with fight/flight reactions. Charles Darwin states, "The word 'fear' seems to be derived from what is sudden and dangerous; and that of terror from the trembling of the vocal organs and body" (289). In Fitzmaurice Voicework no emotion is purely negative, and one is encouraged to allow fear rather than suppress it, since that emotion has a sensitizing effect in developing the radar that warns one of danger. It connects one to the primal survival mechanisms and thereby is the doorway to aliveness. Fear may be expressed vocally through screaming. Yet, in Fitzmaurice Voicework as in bioenergetic therapy, one must be aware that screaming may serve as avoidance rather than a confrontation of fear. Lowen supports this when he writes:

> Fear is more difficult to evoke and more important to elicit. If the
> panic or terror is not brought to the surface and worked out, the
> cathartic effect of releasing the screams, the rage and the sadness
> is short-lived. As long as the patient fails to confront his fear and
> understand the reasons for it, he will continue to scream, cry and
> rage with little change in his overall personality. He will have sub-
> stituted cathartic process for an inhibiting one, but he will not sig-
> nificantly change in the direction of growth. He will remain caught
> between the inhibiting forces he has not understood and worked
> through and the desire to obtain a momentary cathartic release
> (Bioenergetics 121).

Thus *fluffy sound* is offered as an alternative to screaming, as a way for the voice to embody and merge with the fear. Again the keyword is surrender as the voice permits the emotions and fearful sensations to infuse and play through it. Fluffy sound is reflective of and receptive to the tremor, while a scream may push against the fear that is elicited. In tremoring, a fine-tuned sensitization to fear, yielding to the experience of the fear itself rather than mounting a defense against it, is clarified. However, part of the instruction is to surrender a critical mental stance that corresponds with bodily patterns of holding. Therefore, it is important in this work to learn through experimentation via doing rather than censoring. Thus, screaming may be pivotal in some scenarios of recovering the life spark while in others it may be duplicitous, as when the performer indulges, exhibits or overacts. One of the goals of the Voicework is to help the actor in making these distinctions through experimentation in the relative safety of the classroom.

Panic is a further intensification specifically of the fear of suffocation. Lowen elaborates that "Panic is the direct result of the inability to breathe in the face of overwhelming fear" (Betrayal 150). In Fitzmaurice Voicework, it is possible to travel through a destructured realm beyond fight or flight where terror brings one to the brink of paralysis, where one is frozen with fear. In such encounters, it is typical that the student will be encouraged not only to reclaim the ability to breathe and vocalize but to mobilize the body in order to reassert aggressive actions such as kicking or hitting. While such strategies may seem unwelcome or even detrimental, the result can be quite empowering and such resourcefulness, full utilization of the self, and courage to move beyond one's fears may actually support one's creative endeavors by supplying a foundation of confidence. There is also the possibility of deepening understanding of the complexity of the human condition through one's own experience and struggle. In this way, one is prepared for the endeavor of character building as distinguished from character armoring.

Nevertheless, it is important to point out that the Voicework is not invasively probing as some forms of method acting where the actor is confronted and forcibly stripped of defenses. Richard Grossinger sets up a parallel analogy between Reichian therapy and Freudian psychoanalysis:

> In fact, the collaboration of patient and doctor in recovering sources and implicitly sanctifying them is counterproductive in that it encourages the patient to focus on unhappy experiences and gives them [sic] an existential priority in explaining the rest of life. Initially discomfort may be eased by having a lineal cause for compulsion and anxiety, but ultimately the patient becomes so fascinated with his own history, he loses contact with his present somatic reality. The conscious mind becomes its own trap. In place of "psychology," Reich proposed "somatology" – but since mind and body are a unity, these are the same thing" (1: 428).

Distinct from "the method" and aligned to Reichian therapy, the Voicework sets up a space for exploration through physical positions where the actor is invited to navigate an inner world, and although the teacher may initiate as an outer guide, the transference to an inner guide is quickly assumed. In tremoring the wisdom is in the body, and the actor sets the limits of the journey's depth.

Tremor comes from the same etymological root as tremble. Darwin in his study of the emotions notes trembling can be induced by delight, fine music, rage and terror as well as fear (67, 68, 77). Under the rubric of delight comes excitement including that of a sexual nature. The physiological tremor may also be induced in the biological mechanism of shivering when cold as an involuntary response to generate heat. In regard to the tremor, Fitzmaurice lists the following potential benefits:

Release of temporary and chronic tension.

Relaxed but alert mind/brain (alpha waves induced as in meditation).

Reduction of anxiety.

Freer and frequently fuller range of breathing, rhythm, size, placement.

Self-awareness (sensory proprioception).

Sensitizes body to vibration (an aspect of resonance).

Increases energy flow, charge, and presence, with economy of effort (E-mail to the author. 28 Nov. 2005).

In the Voicework, the tremor is seen as a gauge to assess aliveness and is most immediately relevant in the nervous thrill that manifests as stage fright. The Voicework's goal is not to eliminate that fear but to shift it to a response that permits that involuntary reaction so that the energy it elicits is not braced against or suppressed but is liberated as part of the dynamic process of performance. Through tremoring the actor learns to transform reactions of tension to ones that permit energy flow.

FLUFFY SOUND AND DESTRUCTURING

Fluffy sound is the entrance to vocal expression in this system of training. The intent of starting with fluffy sound rather than solid sound or text is to recover the spontaneity of expression at its source prior to the shaping influence of consciousness. In keeping with the quest to reconnect with the deep levels of inner psychophysical awareness and permitting the shift to consciousness without interfering with the actual experience, thus retaining its purity, fluffy sound reflects the emotional and mental content without gripping or managing muscle. Through fluffy sound, in Fitzmaurice Voicework, the focus is on the way one communicates rather than what is communicated in fulfilling the objective of carrying out the action of speech:

> Evidently, therefore, one and the same element of the unconscious, infantile structure is preserved and made manifest in two ways: in what the individual does, says, and thinks; and in the manner in which he acts. It is interesting to note that the analysis of the "what," despite the unity of content and form, leaves the "how" untouched; that this "how" turns out to be the hiding place of the same psychic contents that had already appeared in the "what"; and finally that the analysis of the "how" is especially significant in liberating the affects (Reich, Character 203).

Fluffy sound is appropriate in ascertaining how the person controls, restrains or holds energy. Theoretical basis is found in Lowen: "In bioenergetic therapy there is a constant emphasis on letting the sounds out. The words are less important, though not unimportant. The best sounds are the ones that emerge spontaneously" (Bioenergetics 274). Childhood injunctions that inhibit vocal release are countered in Fitzmaurice Voicework with the permission to sound, and these vibrations are finely tuned to the tremor in order to open the connection between body and voice so that the information contained within the psyche can find outlet. In the destructuring phase, the concept of surrender suggests that fluffy sound precede intentional sound, since by nature it does not require the full closure of the vocal folds. In this introductory stage to sound, the body is speaking without the usual societal controls employed by the mind. There is the sense that the person is journeying back to recover the lost intentions of the body that have been hindered by a variety of social and psychological restraints.

Destructuring, therefore, may elicit memory. Generally, one closes the eyes in order to prompt the inner seeing that enhance the revelation of imagery inherent in the destructuring process. Lowen notes that "In the progression backward from adult to youth to child to infant, one will encounter the reversal that substituted the ego image for the true self" (Pleasure 247). Reich identifies three layers of the psychic structure: the mask, the unconscious, and natural impulse (Function 233). He does this in order to discern those repressive, culturally induced habitual responses that check the core level of primary instinct. Fitzmaurice again employs Reichian therapy to provide a stimulus to the excavating work done to recover the expressive voice and its roots to nature. The process of destructuring presents an arena to contact the fear that has become encoded in the muscular armor of the body that Reich describes, "The character consists in a chronic change of the ego which one might describe as a hardening. This hardening is the actual basis for the becoming chronic of the characteristic mode of reaction; its purpose is to protect the ego from external and internal dangers" (Character 155). The work of dissolving hardness that belongs to destructuring may involve both psychic and physical pain as part of the thawing process. Lowen offers an apt analogy when he describes the pain encountered when a frost bitten finger begins to thaw. It only hurts as it begins to recover (Betrayal 224). This may be termed positive pain in its function to restore vitality to the organism. Lowen points out the "dual aspect" of pain: the function of warning us of danger, thereby constituting a threat to our existence and the prompt "to restore the integrity of the organism" (Pleasure 78-9).

Destructuring itself may be perceived as threatening and causing pain, but it ideally serves as a rite of passage that provides the path through pain to the restoration of joy and pleasure. It should not be confused with the pain itself. Of course, not all pain is positive. For example, the "unpleasure" that Lowen describes which refers back to the orgasm formula (Language 44). It is experienced when the bioelectrical charge becomes great but is not allowed to release. This concept is supported by Pierrakos when he reminds us the origin of the word:

> What creates the tightening and blocking that produces pain? In the Greek language, the word for pain is similar to the words for pathos and passion. Pain is related to desire. And excessive desire does create pain through specific mechanisms of the body and the mind, for the human entity desires and fears pleasure. The desire for pleasure assents to and encourages the flow of the life stream; but the fear of pleasure creates the tightening against the flow of the stream to produce pain. Pain occurs when the entity places itself in a state of tension (125).

The solution to pain that Pierrakos offers conforms to Fitzmaurice in allowing the pain to flow rather than fighting it: "Allowing the free flow of pain permits the divided stream of life to move in one direction. So instead of becoming stuck in a certain area, the stream flows back together and reunifies. The flow can even go in a negative direction instead of a positive one; the pain still would be alleviated because the energy would not be blocked" (Pierrakos 133-4). In the Voicework, tremoring is the procedure used to encounter and counter the pain of tensions caused by ambivalent pulling on the mind, muscles and organs. The tremor as a vibration harmonizes with the vibratory essence of the voice. They are related through their common vibratory aspects to create a potential for fine-tuning body, psyche, emotion and voice into a unity of expression.

In the destructured tremoring mode, one may encounter one's fears in the recovery of one's power through the arousal of the autonomic nervous system that permits an alignment with vocal expressiveness. The tremoring vibrations thus elicited amplify the bioelectricity of the organism and put it back on track with the Reichian orgasm formula leading from tension to relaxation. In the charge phase of tremoring, awareness and sensation is heightened. Lowen provides the thesis that underpins the Voicework when he writes, "When a person becomes charged up, a fine, involuntary tremor or vibration may occur in the legs. This is interpreted as a sign that there is some flow of excitation in the body, specifically in the lower part. The voice may become more resonant since there is more air flowing through the larynx, and the face may brighten" (Bioenergetics 48). Tremoring is a form of personalization in that the actor is gaining self-knowledge in tandem with the intensification of experience. Destructuring utilizes the tremor to transit through the three layers of the psychic structure, the mask or persona, and the unconscious to the core of native impulses. Lowen defines *depersonalization* as "the loss of the feeling of self" (Bioenergetics 51). The concept is antithetically juxtaposed to personalization as inferred by Stanislavski when he advises the student in An Actor Prepares: "Those feelings, drawn from our actual experience, and transferred to our part, are what give life to the play" (155). The tremor, like the spasm, plays out the drama of conflicting energies, the expansive flow of desire and pleasure from the center to the periphery, and the contractive restraint of anxiety from the periphery to the center. But tremoring is the preferred term in the Voicework because a muscle goes into spasm when it cannot get rid of the tension while the tremor has the positive intention of releasing. The actor gains an awareness of self as fluctuations between both the center and the surface of the body set up a wave that has the ability of presenting an assortment of experiences from pleasure to pain. This personal destructuring process taps into a psychophysical range of stimuli and reactions that support the diversity of the actor's resources.

BREATH

Since the primary means of depersonalizing is to restrict moving and breathing (Lowen, Betrayal 82), Fitzmaurice assists the actor through liberation in both of these areas. Lowen provides justification for such assistance when he writes, "Lurking in the background is a feeling of terror perceived consciously as a "strange sensation," against which the organism defends itself by "going dead." In the face of this terror, the body freezes, the breath is held, and all movement stops" (Betrayal 82). In Fitzmaurice Voicework, it is important to understand that terror is supplied by the same basic energy as ultimate pleasure, and, for this reason, the start points are abundant. Thus tremoring offers a technique of personalization that suggests the actor begins in the present, since there is learning in each mental/physical process that serve as entrances to a deeper sense of self. These openings into the self are invariably infused with the breath in this work. Breath harmonizes with tremoring and the voice in its wave-like quality. As tremor, sound and breath move into synchronization; the rhythm conveys the life force that supplies them. Through breath destructured bodies begin to flow in a rhythm that equates to the recovery of primal energies.

In the Voicework, as in bioenergetics, the teacher/guide learns to look for breathing changes in the body as a gauge to how efficacious the process is. Therapeutic insight provides clarity that may further be extended to the physically trapped actor. In a clinical description, Lowen notes, "Generally, as soon as respiration deepens in the schizoid patient, his body begins to tremble and develop clonisms, that is, muscular contractions. Tingling sensations appear in his arms and legs. He begins to perspire. If he becomes frightened at the new sensations in his body, he may become anxious. This anxiety seems related to his fear of losing control or "falling apart."" (Betrayal 149-50). The breathing, which awakens this sense of panic, is also the essential antidote to it. In the Voicework, it is important to distinguish clonus from physiologically induced tremors. It is not the province of the work to treat pathological tremors, the sort that characterizes such diseases as Parkinson. Instead, tremoring is a tool employed by the actor to deepen the potential for expressiveness through aligning the body and mind toward creative release.

Following Reich's orgasm formula, once the body is super charged through tremoring, it is primed for the bioelectric discharge that equates with the creative mode and is supported by the movement of the breath toward energy flow. This is in line with Lowen's observation when he states, "When a patient's breathing is deepened, his tense muscles will go into spontaneous vibration as they become charged with energy. In some patients the vibrations may turn into spontaneous expressive movements as the body itself releases its repressed impulses" (Pleasure 59). Reich calls "the inhibition of respiration...the basic mechanism of neurosis in general". He goes on to explain respiration in terms of its biological function of combustion through its transformation of food to energy. This oxidation process of heating the system up conforms to the orgasm formula by increasing bioelectrical charge:

> Bioelectricity is also produced in this process of combustion. In reduced respiration, less oxygen is introduced, actually only as much as is necessary for the preservation of life. With less energy in the organism, the vegetative excitations are less intense and, there-fore, easier to control. Viewed biologically, the inhibition of respi-ration in neurotics has the function of reducing the production of energy in the organism and, hence, of reducing the production of anxiety (Function 308 – 9).

While Reich offers an explanation for the diminished breathing in the neurotic, he also provides the basis that justifies the goal of destructuring toward a more life-enhanced, sensation charged breath for the actor. In destructuring, a charged breath may lead to discharge in the form of crying. In the Voicework, crying is a form of thawing out. It is an involuntary reaction that heralds that the com-bustive heating of the breath is dissolving the stagnation within held bodies and minds. Fitzmaurice describes grief, an emotion often experienced when crying, as "pressure on the heart" (5th Teacher Certification Program. 15 Jan. 2005) and tears are the result of this release valve. The voice is particularly suited for bioelectri-cal discharge because of its erogenous connection. Dr. Paul J. Moses clarifies that "The organs of speech, from vocal cords to lips, have a discharging function, and the movements of these organs are therefore libidinal in character. In other words, the production of sounds and noises takes place in conjunction with pleasing body sensations" (18). Even the experience of pain finds pleasurable outlet, therefore, in fluffy sound, screaming, and crying when the connection is maintained to vocal release rather than force.

The diaphragm receives a central focus in Fitzmaurice Voicework because it is the main muscle of respiration and it also serves as a barometer of emotional free-dom or stress. This partition that separates the torso between chest and abdomen is metaphorically described by Lowen in a way that is particularly ripe for Voicework analogy:

> In ancient philosophy the body was divided two zones by the diaphragm – the dome-shaped muscle that resembles the contour of the earth. The region above the diaphragm was related to consciousness and the day – that is to the region of light. The area of the body below belonged to the unconscious and the night; it was considered the region of darkness…The belly is symbolically equivalent to the earth and the sea, which are regions of darkness. But it is from these areas, as from the belly, that life comes forth. They are the abode of the mysterious forces involved in life-and-death processes. They are also the abode of the spirit of darkness that dwell in the nether regions. When these primitive ideas became associated with Christian morality, the nether regions were assigned to the devil: the prince of darkness. He lured men to their fall through sexual temptation. The devil dwells in the pit of the earth but also in the pit of the belly where the sexual fires burn. A surrender to these passions could lead to an orgasm in which consciousness becomes dimmed and the ego dissolved, a phenomenon called "the death of the ego." Water is also associated with sex, probably from the fact that life began in the sea. The fear of drowning that many patients connect with the fear of falling can be related to the fear of surrender to sexual feelings (<u>Bioenergetics</u> 222-3).

The central location of the diaphragm figures into the holistic aspect of Fitzmaurice Voicework in the goal of uniting both unconscious and conscious realms. The breath serves as a messenger that is able to traverse physical barriers that segment the psychophysical anatomy. The combustion function of the breath insures that it has the global potential of reaching all cells of the organism. The water symbolism resonates with the state of creative flow that is the Voicework's destination; it is expression filled with receptivity to stimuli.

The breath is never abandoned in this training, for while tremor work is undertaken in the dark, the second phase of the Voicework, restructuring, brings the dark into light. In this phase, the medium of transport is again the breath, now uniting the whole body and infusing intentional communication. Towards this end, Fitzmaurice

47

has coined the phrase "global breath", and there is support for such an idea in bioenergetics when Lowen describes healthy respiration:

> It produces a sensation of flow along the front of the body which ends in the genitals. In healthy breathing the front of the body moves as one piece in a wavelike motion. This kind of breathing is seen in young children and animals, whose emotions are not blocked. Such breathing actually involves the whole body, and tension in any part of the body disturbs this normal pattern. For example, pelvic immobility disrupts this pattern. Normally there is a slight backward movement of the pelvis in inspiration and a slight forward movement in expiration. This is what Reich called the orgasm reflex. If the pelvis is locked in the forward or backward position, this balance-wheel action of the pelvis is prevented (Pleasure 41).

The orgasm reflex, the wavelike motion that characterizes the movement of energy in the body of which breath is a vital part, is utilized also in Fitzmaurice Voicework, although the term more commonly employed is flow. The tremor and the breath have achieved a major goal when the bound energy encountered in rigid patterns of holding is transformed into the fluid movement of the life force. This marks the transition from armoring to flow that will provide the basis for restructuring. Since the transition is dynamic rather than static, it serves too as a learning experience for the actor. How one transitions is of primary concern to the actor whether the shift is from classroom to rehearsal, rehearsal to performance, warm-up to stage, or within a scene in terms of character. In the destructuring phase, one is garnering the tools that can be applied to subsequent transitions in various settings.

Flowing transitions relate to the symbol of the circle in Reichian theory. John Conger notes, "As an ancient symbol of wholeness, the circle became Reich's model of the self" (58). Reich maintained that the orgasm reflex was circular: "In the orgasm, strangely enough, the organism unceasingly attempts to bring together the two embryologically important zones, the mouth and the anus" (Character 366). The orgasm reflex for the Fitzmaurice trained actor becomes a template for fluidity in aligning a continuum of thought and gut motivations. Reich's remarkable insight manifests in the Voicework through the conjunction of the pelvic center as the origin for voice and the mouth as the outlet. This will also figure into Fitzmaurice's employment of chakra imagery. The chakras are dynamic, circular centers for spiritual transformation. The term is derived from yoga. Fitzmaurice utilizes this imagery for aligning a vibrational course through the body starting at the anal or root center and traveling to the expressive or fifth cakra at the throat and mouth. In this anatomical landscape, the diaphragm is the bending mid-point and serves as a transition between the anal and oral end-points. The diaphragm is the center of a breath reflex that rotates the pelvis forward on the outgoing breath and backward on the incoming breath. The breath accompanies the orgasm reflex in a flowing movement that Reich identified by the feeling of surrender (<u>Character</u> 367). Fitzmaurice specifies how she incorporates Reich's reflexes in her work:

> I talk about the breath reflex as the visible (perceivable) flow of movement (energy) through the entire body. I think this is what Reich meant. But one has to discover it oneself. I teach the 'global breath' out to the finger and toenails and the hair, and also call that an amoeba breath, or one cell, or single cell breath in which one <u>becomes</u> rather than <u>does</u> the breathing. One is (pleasurably) overwhelmed by breath. It becomes a habit of self-perception (E-mail to the author. 27 Sept. 2005).

FLOW

Reich identified two different kinds of flow, one belonging to sexuality, distinguished by a pleasurable streaming expanding out from the center of the organism to the periphery, and the anxiety-producing flow that moved in a contractive way from the periphery to the center. The fact that "they are antithetical directions of one and the same excitation process" (<u>Function</u> 267) provides both paradox and solution. This foundational precept Fitzmaurice builds on through the employment of tremoring, breath and fluffy sound to shift bound energy into flow. Elsworth Baker, a colleague of Reich's, offers a definition for Reich's *pleasure streaming* as "The perception of pleasant, wavelike movement of energy in the body much as a soft breeze flowing through. It gives a three-dimensional perception of the body" (xxxiii). This aspect is highlighted in the Voicework as a counterpoise to the often intense personalizing work experienced in destructuring and as an ultimate goal encouraging the pleasurable flow of sound vibrations through the body. In this respect, Lowen notes, "The voice like the body, is a medium through which feeling flows, and when this flow occurs in an easy and rhythmic manner, it is a pleasure both to speaker and listener"

(<u>Pleasure</u> 30). Flow fits into the relaxation portion of Reich's orgasm formula. In the Voicework this materializes as an arrival point where creativity manifests in a fluid, unhampered way.

In addition to the directions of flow from the center to the surface and vice-versa, there is also the directions that move vertically through the body. In bioenergetics these flows are associated with a variety of emotions, as well as the motor and sensory mechanisms. Lowen spins off of Sandor Rado's categories of welfare and emergency emotions in initiating the discussion of directional flow. In the category of the welfare emotions, Rado includes love, sympathy and affection that align with pleasure, while the emergency emotions that are responsive to pain include hate, anger and fear (<u>Pleasure</u> 168). It should be noted that Darwin also documented physical observation of directional flow of emotions throughout <u>The Expression of the Emotions in Man and Animals</u>. According to Lowen, the general flow of direction is such that anger flows up the back, fear down the back, joy up the front and grief down the front. The motor aspect of the nervous system is more dominant in the back and therefore associated with anger and fear, while the sensory aspect has more prominence in the front of the body and therefore is associated with joy and grief. Lowen as Fitzmaurice uses this regional arrangement as a guide in reading the body and not as a hard rule:

> One basic energy motivates all actions. When it charges and flows through the musculature, especially the voluntary muscles, it produces spatial movement which we equate with *aggression* (to move to). When it charged the soft structure such as the blood and skin, it produces sensations which are erotic, tender or loving. Each of these aspects of the emotional life of the individual tends to be localized topographically: the motor component in the back and legs, the sensory component in the front of the body and in the hands. While this tendency to topographical localization is not absolute, for the practical purpose of bioenergetic therapy, this distinction between front and back is valid (<u>Language</u> 91).

Once the actor understands organically and experientially the directions of flow, one can embody character creations that do not adhere to Lowen's natural paths of energy movement. Yet the situation is similar to sublimation, in the sense that the actor has to be free and flowing, i.e., creatively potent before re-directing the energy toward character ends. Otherwise, the actor risks imposing an intellectual construct of character over one's own personal character armor. When dealing with one's own complexity, Fitzmaurice Voicework encourages the actor to start from the present and acknowledge, always through breath and often through action, the various stories that the body tells. Here Fitzmaurice finds support from the Somatic therapist, Stanley Keleman, who identifies the diversity within the human body:

> We have many feelings and they may be in conflict with each other. We can feel sad and angry at the same time. We can want to be friendly and guarded; we can want to reach out to touch and hit simultaneously. A way to experience this is to first feel the complexity of actions and the complexity of feelings, to see where they are located in your body – the anger in the hands, the sadness in the chest, the clinging or hitting in the fingers. Then let that part of the body complete the action. Clench the fist and reach out, lift the chest and put the chest down, let the pelvis reach out sexually, let the jaw look angry. Allow the whole organism to express the different feelings and the different action patterns.
>
> You will find that conflict is not a problem only. It is a source of richness. Being able to live with mixed emotions and mixed feelings is an art, expressing our complexity (39).

In the same way, during tremoring the complex intricacies of the body inform the voice, and in permitting an often-suppressed action, diverse energies when released may begin to harmonize even in their variety to a state of lively flow.

In detailing the directional flow of anger, Lowen notes that aggression is a positive action forward involving the necessary movement of the large muscles of the back and legs. It is also an essential requirement for pleasure: "Aggression is a necessary component of the sexual act for both men and women. In the absence of aggression, sex is reduced to sensuality, to erotic stimulation without climax or orgasm. There is no aggression unless there is an object toward which one moves, a love object in sex, a fantasy object in masturbation" (Bioenergetics 250). Since in Fitzmaurice Voicework, creative energy is the equivalent of sexual energy, many of the exercises used in this work are designed to help restore the aggressive function in the actor.

Fight/flight emotions such as anger and fear are elicited in the Voicework through tremoring. There is a point in destructuring where the emotions move through the body without central nervous system censorship. Both anger and fear figure into the survival mechanism and for the actor can later be applied to the will to win in the scene. Fitzmaurice, in understanding the direction of flow, can, in reading the body, assist the actor through verbal guidance or through touch to bring awareness to physical patterns of restraint, as well as those openings that permit discharge or release. It is significant to this work that one understands the oppositional direction of flows through the anatomy in shifting energy. Fight connected to anger and flight connected to fear are aspects of the same energy, and in shifting the flow through the destructuring series, the actor begins to open up a facility for choice that could support creative decisions. Lowen gives an anatomical picture that fits with Michael Chekhov's psychological gesture in his classic text, To the Actor and with Darwin's exposition when he writes:

> These two opposite directions of movement reflect what happens in the body. The upward movement along the back, which raises the hackles in a dog, together with a forward movement of the head and a lowering of the shoulders is the preparation for assault. The downward movement along the back results in a pulling in of the tail section and the charging of the legs for flight. In a state of fear one turns tail and runs. If flight is impossible, the excitation is caught in the neck and back, shoulders are raised, the eyes are wide open, the head is pulled back, and the tail is tucked in. Since this is the typical expression of fear, this bodily attitude denotes that a person is in a constant state of fear whether he is conscious of it or not (Pleasure 181).

In the destructuring portion of the Voicework, one becomes aware of such tensions and begins to understand, not just intellectually but through experiment and surrender of habitual patterns, how to alter energy flow so that it conforms to the desire of expression rather than repression.

Additionally, by contrast, the tender feelings streaming up along the ventral aspect of the body and emerging through the sensory orifices are especially pertinent to expression. Lowen supports this idea when he writes, "A flow of excitation along the front of the body from the heart to the mouth, eyes and hands will give rise to the feeling of longing expressed in an attitude of opening up and reaching out" (Bioenergetics 52). Energy flow through the heart center is an important stage of the communication path in the Voicework both in the destructuring modality of fluffy sound and in the recovery of words in restructuring. Support is again warranted from Lowen when he writes, "The feelings it gives rise to are tender feelings because the tissues are fluid and soft. The absence of a strong musculature makes this a sensitive region. The energy dominates the structural elements which are mainly vehicles for its movement. Expression of these feelings is mainly by vocal utterance" (Language 84).

The progression of the work is such that it sets the actor up for communication via retrieval of the primal content of reactions, sensation and feelings that now must flow naturally out of the body and into the world. Thus restructuring becomes the logical extension of flow. Reich's early thesis gives the Voicework a prompt when he writes, "On the elementary level, there is but one desire which issues from the biopsychic unity of the person, namely the desire to discharge inner tensions, whether they pertain to the sphere of hunger or of sexuality. This is impossible without contact with the outer world. Hence, the *first* impulse of *every* creature must be a desire to establish contact with the outer world" (Character 270). This Reichian theory suggests the innate need to flow and structure in Fitzmaurice Voicework, for structuring becomes the efficient vehicle for the flow of energetic contacts between self and others:

> Libidinal stretching forth toward the world and narcissistic escape
> from it are merely paraphrases of a very primitive function which
> is present without exception in all living organisms...Turning
> pale with fright, trembling with fear ("hair standing on end")
> correspond to a flight of the cathexis from the periphery of the
> body to the center of the body, brought about by the contraction
> of the peripheral vessels and the dilation of the central vessel sys-
> tem (*anxiety* brought about by stasis). The turgor of the peripheral
> skin tissues, the flushing of the skin, and the feeling of warmth in
> sexual excitation are the exact opposites of this and correspond to
> a physiological as well as psychic flow of the cathexes in direction,
> center → body periphery → world. The erection of the penis and
> the moistening of the vagina are the manifestation of this direc-
> tion of energy in a state of excitation; the shrinking of the penis
> and the becoming dry of the vagina, conversely, are nothing more
> than manifestations of the opposite direction of the cathexes and
> the body fluids from the periphery to the center (Character 275).

In the Voicework, this inner/outer relationship interweaves with sympathetic and parasympathetic nervous responses of fight/flight through tremoring leading to flow and structuring. The idea is to structure with the passion of pleasure.

RESTRUCTURING

At this point the training leads the actor to the critical but exciting prospect of mental, physical and emotional balancing. This is achieved with the departure from the semi-stressful positions on the floor and the return to the dynamic process of standing, which marks an important progression in the work. Grounding is the term used in bioenergetics to identify a person's connection through the feet to nature. In this flowing relationship, there is a continual exchange of energy between the natural body and the earth that supports it. Grounding affirms humanity's connection to the natural realm, a connection that can be challenged in the progression from the instinct run destructured world to a civilized structured one. The transition to standing, in the Voicework, is a significant shift that will be mirrored in the passage from the classroom to the rehearsal hall to the stage. Restructuring ideally comes as the natural extension of the dismantling work done prior to it. Theoretically, it is predicated on the idea that when in touch with the wisdom of natural resources and prompted by natural desires, the actor will recover both the source for creativity and the methods of expression. Since destructuring teaches the actor to honor the interior terrain of impulses, and experiential lessons bring to light the restrictive mechanisms of the past, the actor is primed to allow those insights to lead in the recovery of the functional self that operates in the outer world. The incitement is to maintain the spontaneity of the instincts–to retain a strong linkage to the autonomic nervous response system–while recovering the mental prowess of the central nervous system.

The opportunity here is for the actor to summon the will in conjunction with spontaneity rather than to impose an adversarial relationship between them. This may present the actor with the possibility of a difficult transition because of what Lowen identifies when he writes: "The will is antithetical to pleasure. Its use implies that one is in a painful situation that requires a mobilization of the organism's total resources" (Pleasure 72). Lowen credits Reich with this observation. The tension of employing the will, however, maintains the alert responsiveness of the sympathetic nervous system that in creative endeavors serves an essential function. Significantly, Lowen does acknowledge the necessity of willpower in creative undertakings as well as the human's ability to postpone pleasure in the service of accomplishment. He also admits that work itself can be pleasurable, rhythmical and relaxed. The liberating power of rhythm is uncovered in the tremor, and in Fitzmaurice Voicework, this component is carried over to restructuring both by the rhythmic coordination of the muscles involved in communication and the pleasure of vibrations moving through an energetically flowing body. John Pierrakos, Lowen's colleague and co-founder of Bioenergetic Analysis, distinguishes himself from Reich in emphasizing the positive value of the will:

> All of us continue to focus on the autonomic nervous system, leading the patient through both physical movement and psychoanalytic techniques to release the energy and resolve the character attitudes frozen into the structure of the body and personality. Lowen and I, who began our careers as students and colleagues of Reich, found that while this twofold program is highly effective in itself, it neglected the vital volitional aspect of integral human functioning and proved unable to ensure permanent relief (Core 54).

In bioenergetics and Fitzmaurice Voicework, the ego that employs this "vital volitional aspect of integral human functioning"–the will–has learned new modalities of operation that provide a greater palette for play as information surges out from the inner world of experience based on bodily sensation and feeling. The newly constructed ego then learns to listen to the body as well as the inner images in utilization of the will. The return of the ego is an essential ingredient to restructuring in the outer world. Lowen distinguishes himself from Reich by the restoration of the ego in the healthy psychic structure. While understanding that Reich's concentration on sexuality was prompted by a need to correct the overemphasis on egotistical acquisition of power in Western culture, he also found an unrealistic limit to the continued exclusion of the ego from the treatment model:

> Nevertheless, one cannot go to the opposite extreme of focusing solely on sexuality. This became clear to me after I had unsuccessfully pursued the single goal of sexual fulfillment for my patients, as Reich had. The ego exists as a powerful force in Western man that cannot be dismissed or denied. The therapeutic goal is to integrate the ego with the body and its striving for pleasure and sexual fulfillment (Bioenergetics 30).

Fitzmaurice's restructuring seeks a blend too in asking the actor to rediscover the functions of the ego without losing the integrity of self that comes with grounding that identity in the sensuous soil of the libido. No longer bound physically, or vocally, ideally the actor is free to make choices of communication that pull from a tremendous life source of full orgiastic energies. The Dionysian element is active as the restructured self is animated with a huge potential for bioelectric discharge in creative arenas. Restructuring asks the actor to marry fantasy and imagination with reality as the eyes, usually closed in destructuring, open to see the outer world. Fitzmaurice clarifies her position and identifies the marks of an actor proficient in her approach when she notes:

> An actor trained in Fitzmaurice Voicework makes no separation between the acting process and his voice. (If the audience is aware of the voice it's usually because it's a block to rather than a vehicle of communication, even, perhaps especially, when the voice is considered good). I want the voice to convey the imagination, feelings, and thoughts of the actor, with an expressive range of sound qualities as well as with the more technical aspects of range, of pitch, volume, and rate/rhythm. The actor will be coming from his physical/metaphysical centre by engaging the transverse to speak, rather than by squeezing, by aiming for emotional effect, or by sounding uniform and dull. He will not be merely aiming for an effect through sound, but his mind and intentions are active through use of the focus line. The speech is audible, clear, and easily modifiable according to the particular textual and space demands, and doesn't intrude unnecessarily as good theatre speech. Singing isn't a separate and unwelcome or scary task. The actor trusts his instincts and impulses, has clear and personal images, knows how to structure and arc text, scenes, plays, and characters. He is able to take responsibility for his own work, while being in full communication and appropriate interaction with fellow actors, the director, and ultimately the audience (E-mail correspondence to the author. 29 Apr. 2006).

In the transmission between eye and world, the leitmotifs of aggression and surrender are operative. Aggression, in the original sense as intended by Lowen of moving toward, by coupling with the receptivity integral to the act of seeing, maintains the principle of balanced flow recovered through tremoring. If the tremoring has achieved its goal, then the sensory organs, including sight, are heightened as energy flows in both directions through the eyes. Thus, the external world and all the myriad of images that travel in through the eye, move into an embrace with the inner images that have welled up from the destructured realms. Inner and outer vision dialogue and join in a transaction with alternating transmission and reception. These transactions form a union that is parallel to the sexual one put forth by Reich as a template for vitality. Further, this template for orgastic potency informs the voice. While words may be utilized in destructuring, they are mandatory in the return to this outer world. This balance of words and instincts may be seen as a big challenge but it is also the ultimate evolutionary process that promises extraordinary pleasure, moving the communication beyond the ordinary restraints of censor run speech and beyond the unbridled outbursts of raw emotion to the unity incumbent upon the powerful being that Lowen calls a "cultured animal" (Pleasure 250). As opposed to the creatively subdued domesticated animal's separation from self, it is the dynamic 'fusion' between wisdom and play occurring within this cultured animal that the Fitzmaurice training goes toward in restructuring.

On the other hand, restructuring is not a static idyllic state without tests. It is an addition to, rather than the elimination of the complexity encountered in destructuring. Reich notes that, "the human structure is animated by the contradiction between an intense longing for and fear of freedom" (Mass 322). If, as Reich states, this is a fact of the human condition, it is a particularly useful insight for the actor given to grappling with the conflicts intrinsic to dramatic art. In recognition of humanity's quandary, it is essential to retain the dynamic energy elicited through fight and flight as one transitions on to the heightened and sophisticated modalities of words and character. In such a transaction, the actor learns that relying on the limits of one's own character structure is not equivalent to creating a character. The potential of a humbling effect is implicit in the empowerment that goes with destructuring if the compassion for self that is awakened can be extended to others. Unfolding one's own mechanisms for survival, coping and defending may lead to a broader view of humanity that fuels the intentions an actor might play in creating character. If the destructuring process proceeded effectively, there is considerable energy available that previously held by tensions is now freed to contribute to the choices of restructuring based on various uses of self in service of illuminating other characters. The facts of human life that one comes to know through destructuring constitute a reality principle in maintaining connection with the body and its visceral gut reactions that lend an authenticity to character creations. The Voicework makes a palpable connection to Lowen's theory when he writes, "The first step toward reality taken by the patient is his identification with his body... This identification with the body is also the first step toward self-realization" (Pleasure 248-9). This reality principle also extends itself when the actor interfaces with the demands of the outer world and responds by structuring communicative responses. The proficient balancing between technical learned behavior that is elicited through contact with the exterior and instinctive gut behavior constitutes the creative reality sought after in the Voicework. In practical terms, this manifests as the need for more oxygen to supply the task of communication. In addition, therefore, to the diaphragmatic breath that served in destructuring, the greater need elicits the response of the intercostals and the supportive activation of the transverses.

The breath is involved in many areas of restructuring. The liberated destructured breath, for example, nourishes the organs of perception used in the restructuring phase: "Breathing has a positive effect on the eyes. After sustained deep breathing through the various exercises the eyes of most patients are noticeably brighter. Patients themselves often comment on their improved vision, as I mentioned earlier. Grounding exercises also help this process" (Lowen, Bioenergetics 291). The nourishing of the eye function with breath stimulates alertness that enhances the flow of energy that Fitzmaurice maps as commencing in the navel center, traveling down to the pelvic region and then streaming up parallel to the spine to emerge out of the area between the eyebrows, an area called the third eye in the yogic tradition. She calls this line of energy *focus point* when it arrives at its destination in the outer world. The grounding in the pelvic center, the metaphorical dark world of strong drives with the sensory connection to the earth via the feet, assure that the geographically more distant eye region and the cerebrally linked ego are not isolated from the full body experience.

The sensuality of seeing is restored in the focus-line. Elsworth Baker notes that, "Excitation from the eyes is felt directly in the genital as a pleasurable thrill... Through the eyes, the environment actually becomes an extension of the individual so that awareness of it is the same as awareness of his own body; yet at the same time he clearly distinguishes between the two, learning to pinpoint pleasurable and painful areas with unfailing accuracy" (19). Eye and ego are related etymologically, as Pierrakos notes when he states, "The word *ego* comes from the Greek roots: e meaning

"I", and *go*, the contraction of the term for "earth". Numerous metaphysical traditions consider the I to be analogous to the physical eye and seek to develop themselves
through the faculty of sight. In a sense, the ego represents the eye on earth, which
perceives and interprets reality" (116). It is equally relevant that both eye and ego are
recovered and restructured with the assistance of the breath, for the respiration is a
tangible link to the primal instincts, the natural impulses. When infused with the
flow of destructured feelings, the focus-line serves as a junction for the re-entry of the
discriminating function of the ego in managing the current of thought, breath and
voice without domination. The focus-line also serves as a point of merger between the
communicator and the listener. In this way, the union attained in communication
via sound and speech again parallels the sexual union that is the flourishing hallmark
of Reich's orgasm formula. Thus vocal expression, following the Fitzmaurice strategy, achieves the pleasurable union that fulfills human potential in Reichian therapy,
both in the joining of the autonomic nervous system with the central nervous system
within the speaker and in the flow of energetic exchange between the speaker and the
listener.

MORAL CONSIDERATIONS

In a larger sense, beyond the individual, Reich was advocating a total revo-
lutionizing of the psychology within the socio-political structure. While Reich's
theories are often cited as a justification for sexual licentiousness, and although he
is often credited as the inspirational spearhead of the sexual liberation movement of
the 1960s, it must be emphasized that his ideology has a strong moral underpinning.
Reich attacks the 'compulsive morality' dictated and imposed by patriarchal govern-
ment and religious organizations (Function 11). He argues that sexual repression is
fundamentally sociological and not biological (Function 229). But he then posits an
alternative, the recuperation of an innate moral core that is housed within human
beings. This natural morality, he believed, would come forth once the birthright of
orgastic potency is restored to humanity. "Moralistic bigotry cannot be fought with
another form of compulsive morality, but only with knowledge of the natural law of
the sexual process. Natural moral behavior presupposes that the natural life process
can develop freely. On the other hand, compulsive morality and pathological sexuality go hand in hand" (Function 18). Reich asserts that inherent to the make-up
of a sexually potent being, is the ability to self-regulate the passions (Function 181).

Delving beyond the troubled unconscious fraught with negative, neurotic tendencies, Reich demonstrates considerable confidence in humanity's resourcefulness for constructive life when he writes: "If one penetrates through this destructive second layer, deeper into the biologic substratum of the human animal, one always discovers the third, deepest layer, which we call the *biologic core*. In this core, under favorable conditions, man is an essentially honest, industrious, cooperative, loving, and if motivated, rationally hating animal" (Mass xi). This essentially optimistic credo reflects in the Voicework theory that maintains an innate progression from destructuring to spontaneous restructuring, if one proceeds with sufficient depth into the process.

Ultimately, the problem with Reich's morality, as with the dictates that he sought to efface, was that it too hit a wall in setting up a prescribed code of behavior. The risk morality runs is that it rigidifies into a system based in categorical imperatives. Richard Grossinger notes, in his overview of Reichian therapy that, Although it diametrically contradicted his intention, Reich set a standard of absolute orgastic potency against which men and women had to measure their own shortcomings. Reich said, in effect: most people are ruined from early childhood and will never know "the real thing." This was a quintessential power play, and its consequence is a legacy of "feeling" elitists, and promiscuous orgasm-seekers, all looking for the perfect wave and claiming to be his children (1: 441).

This kind of morality is intrinsically exclusive. Reich did, of course, criticize Freudian analysis as basically catering to the privileged classes, but he never deviated much from Freud on the issue of sexual preference. For example, it is questionable that his morality would welcome sexual orientations other than heterosexual into the fold. Because the demands of Reich's theories were so absolute, he was not able to reconcile them with the actual reality of daily life and ultimately abandoned his enthusiastic belief in human redemption. In this, he came to share Freud's pessimism:

> He (Freud) gave up before he started. I came to the same conclusion, but only after much experience and failure. Nothing can be done with grownups...Once a tree has grown crooked, you can't straighten it...He (Freud) was disappointed, clearly disappointed. And he was right. Nothing can be done. Nothing can be done (Higgins and Raphael 70).

Lowen, in developing bioenergetics from Reichian theories, attempts to democratize these absolute precepts by tempering the primacy of sexual fulfillment with ego needs and the acceptance of humanity's complex emotional life. Grossinger notes a key distinction:

> The basic difference, for instance, between the Reichian orthodoxy and the offshoot bioenergetic tradition associated with Alexander Lowen and his disciples is that the emphasis on orgastic performance is replaced, in bioenergetics, by more attention to pure feeling. Feeling means subtlety, tolerance, range. It means living somatically in the world as it is, experiencing all different sorts of emotions which are *also* energetically cleansing and curative (1: 441).

Further, in the aftermath of Reich, John Pierrakos sees his unique contribution as the inclusion of spiritual development and heart centrality: "After many years of bioenergetic work, I came to feel that something was lacking. Though bioenergetics provided a beautiful clinical approach to resolving blocks, difficulties, and neurotic symptoms, it lacked a fundamental philosophy because it did not incorporate the spiritual nature of human beings" (276). To this end, Pierrakos included the reading of auras and the exaltation of love over orgastic potency in his therapeutic model. These later ramifications and deviations influenced Fitzmaurice, who as an acting teacher, recognized the need to maintain an open mind and in her work sought to synthesize all these distinct contributions in honoring the complexity and variety of choices that the performer is called on to make. She does not limit herself to an ideological stance but maintains a fluid tenure with permeable junction points in order to keep her work vital.

In addition to these well-known therapists, Fitzmaurice also shares an affinity with somatic psychologist, Stanley Keleman. His discussion of 'middle ground' supports the Voicework's need to operate as a live system of training, which means a system that, while having a core of unifying principles, is open to interrogation and change by its very nature. Keleman details a creative location that intersects with the Voicework when he writes:

> Middle Ground follows an ending. There is a pause, a swelling, a tremendous flood of mixed emotions, sensations and dreams of the

future. It is a transitional phase, a no man's land, the cauldron of our biological process out of which we can form a new connection. This slowing down, this pause in middle ground is like a dream state where there are positive and negative feelings that come out of the shadows, as if being lit by a strobe light. Things are out of sequence and there is no sense of recognizable connectivity.

The middle ground is like an ocean welling up with images, sensations, feelings and needs, each taking its turn on the stage, asking clamoring for attention, trying itself out in the field of consciousness so we can then use it in the social world. Things aren't rational. Time isn't ordered. Gravity is upside down. Middle grounds are androgynous, bisexual. This realm of our inner world is both masculine and feminine; it is a womb where the newly conceived gestates (77-8).

This multi-gendered world of potentials dovetails with Fitzmaurice Voicework via tremoring that opens a 'middle ground' between events, a kind of Checkovian universe of perpetual flow and transitions. Exploration here provides tools for living and, when applied to the theater, living in the moment creatively. In regard to moral impositions, Fitzmaurice clarifies her position when she states:

I see personality changes, but I don't set up to create them. I might perhaps use language around finding centre, balance, and responsiveness instead of reactivity or agenda. I think the balanced energies reduce antisocial behaviors, and competitiveness except for fun. You could say a natural morality is perhaps implied, but it isn't a stated goal. I don't impose a structure, ethics or otherwise except for the logistics of time and sequential learning (E-mail correspondence to the author. 27 Sept. 2005).

Reich's complex relationship to morality is paralleled in the scenario that emerges from his stance on mysticism. In spite of his numerous objections to religious mysticism, Reich's later theories took a decidedly mystic bent. In order to understand the complex weaving of the Voicework with such metaphysical traditions as yoga and shiatsu, it is important to regard the Reichian contribution to the discussion.

Reich *himself* asserted that he was a scientist and vehemently stated that he was anti-mystical. This can be evidenced in such statements as, "An individual who is sexually happy does not need an inhibiting 'morality' or a supernatural 'religious experience.' Basically, life is simple as that. It becomes complicated only by the human structure which is characterized by the fear of life" (Sexual 269). Reich investigated the link between religious and sexual ecstasy, concluding that the religious devotee who surrendered to the church, or to the notion of some cosmic entity, was essentially in a state of perpetual sexual frustration. According to Reich, the oppression of religious doctrine was anti-life in its denial of earthly pleasure. Reich takes on mysticism as a substitute for healthy pleasurable encounter when he writes:

> It is known from the treatment of mentally sick priests that an involuntary ejaculation often occurs at the height of religious ecstasy. Normal orgastic gratification is replaced by a general condition of physical excitation, which excludes the genitals and, as if by accident, brings about a partial release against one's will...The deep longing for redemption and release – *consciously* from "sins" *unconsciously* from sexual tensions – is warded off. States of religious ecstasy are nothing other than conditions of sexual excitation of the vegetative nervous system, which can never be released (Mass 148-9).

Yet, in spite of his objections, Reich's own theory that posited the redemption of a natural morality was easily configured into a mystical proposition by many of his followers.

One of his followers, Lowen, viewed mysticism and mechanism as two sides of the same coin:

> I believe we are now in a position to understand the problem of mysticism vs. mechanism. Both attitudes are the result of an armored state. The mystic lives in the inner world and has dissociated himself from the events in the outer...The mechanist, who is on the other side of the wall, has lost contact with his center. All he sees is how he reacts to events in a causal way, and so he believes life is merely a matter of conditioned reflexes. Since objects and events determined his reactions, his energies are committed to manipulat-

ing an environment which he senses is alien and hostile to his being
(<u>Bioenergetics</u> 310).

He reconciled mystical and mechanical propensities in the therapeutic process
of connecting head consciousness to body consciousness. In expanding the
consciousness, Fitzmaurice Voicework starts from the body too. While the Voicework
may resonate with spirituality, it retains its grounding in bodily sensations and physical experiences that give it a practical application for theater work. Nonetheless,
Fitzmaurice is not averse to admitting the spiritual connotations implicit to her work,
and in this she finds kinship with Pierrakos.

Pierrakos, building on Reich's concept of a "biologic core" and preserving his
earlier optimism, openly acknowledged the spiritual significance of his therapeutic
modality by emphasizing an inner journey that has mystical overtones:

> The core is the human being's whole capacity, a glowing, vital mass,
> both the source and the perceiver of life force. The core has com-
> plete unity. No duality exists at this first level of reality, no either-
> or, no good-bad. It is an indivisible vibratory operation, a process
> in which every person knows the truth instinctively by sensing the
> pulse of life. The qualitative characteristics of the core's movements
> are the primal positive emotions, or movements to make contact
> and unity with the outside world. These can be summed up as one
> supreme expression: love (25).

Fitzmaurice, maintaining porosity to her work, seeks to blend the multiple aspects
of the self by developing awareness of a strong center in conjunction with a powerful desire to interact with the outside. In this work, expansion of consciousness goes hand in hand with depth of perception as destructuring supplies density
of texture for vocal communication while vision so endowed permits sensuous
seeing.

Reich's antireligious fervor did not exclude the East. Most relevant to this study,
he objected to the asceticism of yoga. In regarding the ideological debate between
Reich and the East, it is important to note how the Voicework, which pulls from both
cultures, reconciles the theoretical adversity. While it can be argued that Fitzmaurice
picks and chooses among these various systems and that she is justified in doing so as
an actor and as an expert teacher of actors, it is also interesting to fathom the subtle

intricacies and the revolutionary selections that create a philosophical weaving for her work. First, Reich's apparent protestations to Eastern doctrine must be examined. Many of his criticisms were aimed against the concept of *nirvana*, commonly considered a Buddhist term but conceptually present in yogic philosophy too in the concept of *moksha* i.e. liberation or release. "Conscious longing for death, peace, nothingness ("the nirvana principle"), occurs only under the condition of hopelessness and the absence of sexual, in particular genital, gratification. It is, in short, the manifestation of complete resignation, a retreat from a reality which had become *solely* unpleasurable into nothingness" (Character 278).

In another statement that focuses on Christianity, he saw a "masochistic mechanism" that extended to the ascetic yogi, operating in the devotee's endurance of suffering. He equated such a quest for painful denial as "the loss of the organic capacity" for life affirming pleasure (Function 256). Additionally, Reich viewed concepts of transcendence as forms of masked repressions: "What happened is this: Originally, one condemned sensuality; but the repressed forces returned, in all kinds of pathological forms. What was to be done with these forces which now, even more than before, conflicts with a "moral" i.e., ascetic and chaste way of living? Only one thing was left: 'lifting sexuality to a higher spiritual plane'" (Sexual 42). Although he doesn't mention the Hindu practice, his criticism could relate to tantric yoga as a form of repression under the guise of lifting sexual intercourse to a higher level.

To his credit it should be noted that Reich's critical stance was not impelled by a desire to institute draconian measures but to emancipate humanity from what he perceived as moral/mystical strait jackets. It must be stressed, also, that Reich, like Fitzmaurice, embraced a philosophy that relished life in all its complex abundance. Fitzmaurice overlaps with Reich in welcoming life in all its turmoil, complexity and fullness. Perhaps this marks one of the distinctions that align training for the actor with bioenergetics against more predominately religious or spiritually based pursuits. Toward this end, Reich not only rejected yogic philosophy but a slew of other 'isms':

> Psychic health is characterized, not by the Nirvana theory of the
> Yogis and the Buddhists, the hedonism of the epicureans, the
> renunciation of monasticism; it is characterized by the alterna-
> tion between unpleasurable struggle and happiness, error and
> truth, deviation and rectification, rational hate and rational love;

in short, by being fully alive in all situations of life" (Function 201).

In his passionate support of the life force, Reich was against any structure of thought that minimized or rejected the capacity to experience. In this basic idea, Fitzmaurice builds a bridge to him. Unburdened by any proscriptions of mystical constraints, Fitzmaurice seeks to give the actor a larger dimension of truth not by denial but by experience, and if the actor is led to a mystical awakening, it grows out of the soil of sensation, play and permission rather than renunciation.

COSMIC CONNECTION

Reich specified that: "Mysticism here means, in a literal sense, a change of sensory impressions and organ sensations into something unreal and beyond this world" (Ether 78) and sought to disassociate himself from that designation. Nevertheless, Reich, a professed scientist, would come to acknowledge a cosmic connection in his theories about the orgasm, and while he continued to see an antithesis between science and mysticism, his work, in spite of his intentions, would plant the seeds for links to spirituality that would both inform bioenergetics and Fitzmaurice Voicework. Reich's situation is similar to that of the quantum physicists who were linked, sometimes against their will, to Eastern cosmology. It can be argued that his scientific experiments, albeit with laboratory apparatus, such as amplifiers, silver electrodes, and electron tubes, hailed back to alchemical roots and still contained a highly metaphysic element that would create an affinity to spiritual seekers that experimented in the human laboratory with meditation, contemplation, devotion and physical abstinence.

A radical change for Reich came when, while observing fluid movement, he began to question the idea of a mechanical mind/body connection. Instead, he posited the possibility of some essential entity beyond psychological phenomena that causes the movement of life:

> The crucial problem of orgastic impotence was still unsolved: it is possible for the genital organs to be filled with blood without a trace of excitation. Hence, sexual excitation can certainly not be identical with, nor be the expression of the flow of blood...In addition to the flow of blood, there must be something else which, depending upon its biological function, causes anxiety, anger, or pleasure. In

this process, the flow of blood merely represents an essential means. Perhaps this unknown "something" does not occur when the movement of the body fluids is hindered (<u>Function</u> 272).

Later, Reich would pin down this mysterious "something", identifying it first as bio-electricity (<u>Function</u> 272) and then through further experiments as *orgone*: "It was demonstrated that the sun emits an energy which influences rubber and cotton in the same manner in which it influences the bion culture and the human organism after full respiration in a vegetatively undisturbed state. I called this energy which is capable of charging organic matter, orgone" (<u>Function</u> 383). In clarifying the significance of his finding, Reich defines his neologisms further:

> At this point, the investigation of the living organism went beyond the boundaries of depth psychology and physiology; it entered unexplored biological territory. For the past five years, the investigation of the *bion* has absorbed all available attention. The "bions" are microscopic vesicles charged with orgone energy; they are developed from inorganic matter through heating and swelling. They propagate like bacteria. They also develop spontaneously in the earth or, as in cancer, from decayed organic matter (<u>Function</u> 383).

Thus, the term 'bion', having cosmological and metaphysical connotations becomes the foundation on which bioenergetics is built. Such connotations, whether Reich intended them or not, opens up the system based on his work, bioenergetics, to the possibility of mystical interconnections.

Dealing with the nature of the life force, he shares a border with spiritual ideologies, and at times it is difficult to maintain the integrity of those boundaries. It should be noted, of course, that Reich did not align himself with any spiritualist tradition in his findings, and he professed that the energy he had identified was visible and measurable. Yet he could not find validation or endorsement from the scientific community he sought approval from, and his orgone theory is generally considered unproven and unconventional. Reich, however, did not seek any compensatory camaraderie with the Eastern traditions. Nevertheless, orgone energy, regardless of the methods Reich employed to discover it, shares a sympathetic correlation to such yogic and

Taoist concepts as *prana* and *qi* through their common denominator as underlying universal life forces:

> We cannot, on the other hand, put into words the expressive movements of the living organism which do not belong specifically to the living but are projected into this sphere from the sphere of the non-living. Since the living derives from the non-living and the non-living material derives from cosmic energy, we are justified in concluding that there are cosmic energy functions in the living. Hence, it is possible that the untranslatable expressive movements of the orgasm reflex in the sexual superimposition represent the sought-for cosmic orgone functions (<u>Character</u> 394).

In this, Reich links heavenly bodies to earthly bodies including human ones. Further, by equating "cosmic longing" with the desire for orgastic release, he is no longer saying that religious ecstasy is a poor substitute for sexual ecstasy but justifiably a natural impulse springing from a common origin:

> I am well aware of the magnitude of this work hypothesis. But I see no way of avoiding it. It has been clinically established that orgastic longing, i.e., yearning for superimposition, always goes together with cosmic longing and cosmic sensations. The mystical ideas of innumerable religions, the belief in a Beyond, the doctrine of the transmigration of the soul, etc., derive, without exception, from cosmic longing; and, functionally, the cosmic yearning is anchored in the expressive movements of the orgasm reflex. In the orgasm, the living organism is nothing but a part of pulsating nature (<u>Character</u> 394).

If "cosmic longing" is the bottom line, then humanity's quest becomes exalted. Sublimation, in this context, takes on its archaic meaning, having majestic connotations that suggest lifting humanity beyond the threshold and bonds of limitation toward metaphysical union. Orgone energy becomes sublime when Reich states: "Yet there lives and thrives in us a thirst for knowledge stronger than any philosophical thought, be it life-positive or life-negative. This burning urge to know can be felt like a stretching out of our senses beyond the material framework of our body, enabling us to understand what is rational in the metaphysical view of existence" (<u>Cosmic</u> 278-9).

While he may not be relenting on the primacy of orgastic potency, he has opened a door where dialogue becomes permissible between physical and spiritual longing.

Fitzmaurice Voicework and bioenergetics grow from this dialogue with the aim to develop into complete systems that address physical, mental, emotional and spiritual fulfillment in the human organism. The common intersection is that they are systems of recovery, and in this there will be further porosity to the Eastern disciplines discussed in the next chapter. The specific orientation of the Voicework is creative and artistically inclined, but there are deep interfaces with therapeutic recovery that can also be seen in the transactions with yoga and shiatsu.

CHAPTER THREE:
INTERSECTIONS EAST

INTRODUCTION: EXPLORING THE BORDERLANDS

With regard to further influences on Fitzmaurice Voicework, it must be acknowledged that they came after she had already established her work as a fully functional system. Whereas bioenergetics may be considered a primary influence, yoga and shiatsu were secondary. Their secondary influence did not, however, relegate them to second-class status within the Voicework, as their theoretical underpinnings soon grew significant attachments to the bioenergetic roots already present within her method. Her work had ripened to a point where it asked for such unions to propel it forward to its next level of evolution. This communicative quality characterizes the Voicework as a vital, growing system rather than as one that rigidifies into proscriptive codifications. The three systems, Fitzmaurice Voicework, yoga and shiatsu, of course, retain their integrity and unique identity in these unions. In this way, mergers are possible but so are disagreements. For instance, she retains the integrity of the bioenergetic blueprint within the postures, looking for intersections within yoga asanas or shiatsu meridian theory while keeping a clear perspective on the actor oriented intentions of those positions. Yet, there are currents of thought that are so congruent that the junctures offer the opportunity for a profound East/West synthesis.

Since the recent influx of Eastern esoteric culture in the West, scholarly circles often address the question of appropriation. Many voice teachers, for example, borrow yoga postures and utilize them in their classes. Fitzmaurice does not affix or borrow so much as creates a space for fluid dialogue between systems. Compared to other currently popular approaches to voice training for actors in America, Fitzmaurice Voicework is most unique in the depth of this East/West dialogue. What this chapter will look at is these theoretical points of convergence and distinction in order to grasp the Voicework's overall design in a fuller holistic frame. The author of <u>Science Studies Yoga</u>, James Funderburk, gives justification for maintaining an open mind to such inevitable intercultural exchanges:

> The reasons for reversal in attitude are many. The expanding speed
> and depth of communications have provided us occidentals with
> an increasing understanding of the philosophic foundations of
> yoga and meditation. Jet travel and changing political attitudes
> have fostered the means for direct exchanges of information. Many
> Americans have been able to observe directly the yogic and medita-
> tion practices of India, while teachers and yoga masters from India
> have been able to establish important educational centers in the
> West. (xii-xiii)

If Funderburk's argument is valid for the late 1970's, the technology of a computer
driven information highway in subsequent decades has reinforced it further. While
purists on both sides of the exchanging cultures may wish to stem the tide, the inevi-
tability of cross-disciplinary studies must be acknowledged, and these jointures profit
from careful assessment rather than dismissal. Clearly, Fitzmaurice does not lay any
claim to being a yoga teacher. She honors yoga's sanctity in preserving an ancient
culture while locating in the evolution of her own work natural ties to that culture.
But she also recognizes the currency of yoga that marks it too as a growing, evolving
system and looks at those points of convergence for illumination to further enhance
vocal freedom for the actor. The details of these transactions when carried out in the
spirit of humility act as a balance to the quest for knowledge. One of the questions
that will be addressed is how Fitzmaurice walks this fine tightrope between cultures
in a system that is fundamentally concerned with the development of the actor's creative spirit through vocal expression.

In a general sense, through just engaging in these dynamic, experimental mergers, Fitzmaurice is summoning the spirit of yoga, for yoga means union. There is also
a primary yogic thread that runs through her work even before the move toward the
East. This is already manifested in the synthesis inherent in her work through the
dualities of destructuring and restructuring. These provide a harmonic evocation of
balance between opposites that fits with the very meaning of yoga. Obviously, from
the inception of the comparison, however, a critical distinction must be made, for as
B.K.S. Iyengar points out in regard to yoga, "It is the true union of our will with the
will of God" (Light on Yoga 19). Further theoretical dissention comes from Reich, in
his early assessments, when he adamantly opposed what he viewed as the mystical
basis of yoga, and his objection suggests an irreconcilable ideological inconsistency.

While one might argue that Fitzmaurice Voicework is moving the actor toward a more specifically worldly than mystical union, a strict adherence to the privileging of spirituality would tend to present an impassable barrier between this voice system and yoga. Lowen, in this respect, confirms this important delineation between bioenergetics and yoga based on spiritual orientation:

> I had looked into yoga before I met Reich, but it did not appeal to my Western mind. Yet through my work with Reich I was aware of some similarity between the practice of yoga and Reichian therapy. In both systems the main emphasis is on the importance of breathing. The difference between the two schools of thought was in their direction. In yoga the direction is inward toward spiritual development; in Reichian therapy it is outward, toward creativity and joy. A reconciliation of these two views is surely needed, and it is my hope that bioenergetics can help (<u>Bioenergetics</u> 72).

Thus, while locating an essential distinction, Lowen also identifies a void that Fitzmaurice Voicework, due to its association with bioenergetics, is invited to fill as part of a reconciliatory project. Because of the inner/outer dimensionality of the Voicework training through destructuring and restructuring with its resonating symbolism of conjoining opposites, it is favorably poised to tackle this task. For just as Pierrakos, one of Fitzmaurice's teachers, went on to openly avow the significance of spirit and heart centrality, thus moving beyond Reichian body/mind based therapy, Fitzmaurice, also, opens her approach in this direction in order to define a more holistically, multi-dimensional actor. Spirit, of course, is not lacking in the Voicework, as it is present in any artistic pursuit. But with all due respect to the reverent tone set down by Iyengar, it is another definition of yoga that is potentially more open to Voicework comparisons and it is to this interpretation that the Voicework will most adhere. Because yoga is an ancient but living art, it also allows an evolving trajectory, and a broader interpretation than Iyengar's points the way to a cohesive harmony between the two approaches:

> The word *yoga* comes from the Sanskrit root *yuj*, which means "to yoke." This means that the lower levels of consciousness, the lower aspects of oneself, are yoked to the higher center of consciousness so that they become guided, directed and regulated by it. They become tools in the hands of the higher consciousness. When this

is one's underlying orientation, then diverse schools of training and various disciplines can be employed when appropriate to serve the user (Rama, Ballentine, and Ajaya 284).

While the tone of the semantics of this quote may not entirely jibe with Voicework's terminology and must be interrogated through further examination, the suitable permission for exchange is explicit in this expansive view of yoga. The quote mirrors the two phases of the Voicework, with lower consciousness related to destructuring and higher consciousness paralleling the principles of restructuring.

Yoga is a dense psycho-spiritual technology with many forms:

Within the realm of Hinduism, six major forms of Yoga have gained prominence. They are Raja-Yoga, Hatha-Yoga, Jnana-Yoga, Bhaki-Yoga, Karma-Yoga, and Mantra-Yoga. To these must be added Laya-Yoga, and Kundalini-Yoga, which are closely associated with Hatha-Yoga but are often mentioned as independent approaches. These two are also subsumed under Tantra-Yoga (Feuerstein 28).

Fitzmaurice Voicework dialogues most readily with hatha-yoga, kundalini-Yoga, and tantra-Yoga. The extent of this study will be limited to the Voicework's linkage with these forms of yoga, which all make provision for meditation, breath control and physical postures.

In the sense that *ha / tha* correspond to sun and moon respectively, the word reinforces the union of dualities that concretizes the common ground with Fitzmaurice Voicework's destructuring and restructuring. Extending the sun/moon duality of yoga further, one can also see in it the goal of mind/body unity that it shares with Fitzmaurice work. Both move away from the typical Cartesian mind/body dichotomy in that they are systems involving synthesis. "From the standpoint of Yoga theory, mind, and body always function as one organic whole. Intellectual and emotional processes are regarded in much the same way as physiological and structural ones – as material processes" (Kraftsow, <u>Wellness</u> 301). This sounds strongly like Reich when he talks of the functional identity between psyche and soma (<u>Char. Analysis</u> 351). Yoga theory, seeking a universal unification, thus views all material manifestations as one. This all-encompassing perspective also strongly resonates with Reich's latter cosmic self when he elaborated his theory of orgone energy. Here two paths originating from opposite East/West directions find intersection in a territory that provides fertility to nourish the Voicework. Bioenergetics growing out of Reichian therapy, the Voicework, and yoga are all psychophysical techniques:

> As we have seen, this process is most succinctly summarized in terms of observation, control and synthesis: growth is always based on the attainment of some degree of disentanglement from attachments, which allows one to observe something about himself and his world to which he was previously blind. This is the expansion of awareness. As awareness grows, one inevitably discovers within his new definition of himself a new ability to control. What he was previously blind to and controlled by is now within his power to regulate. Increased capacity for observation leads to increased capacity to control. We've seen how this principle applies in working with the body, in working with the mind, as well as in working on other levels (Rama, Ballentine, and Ajaya 281).

Since the choice of words used in instruction can have either a liberating or limiting effect, it is important to acknowledge that the words used in the citation above are not equivalent to the ones used in the Voicework. In looking at the Voicework and yoga systems, it is important not to equate them. The point is not to iron out all the differences in terminology but to find out how to live in the borderland between these distinctions. Part of the demand of hybridity is creating a new identity and a new synthesis based on an open dialogue rather than on absolute agreement. The not-so-neat junctures are equally as profitable as those areas of overlap because of the lessons learned in clarifying and defining the space between contacts. In this way, the potential is set in motion for a larger expressiveness, subtlety, and a greater possibility of resources when acting. One expands through grappling with the disconnections as well as arriving at the points of firm accord. The actor who chooses to open up a larger field of play profits from such exchanges through expanding awareness and literally increasing sound and movement vocabularies. The target readership, in this respect, is the actor who does yoga and the yogi who acts. The question of reconciliation is an ongoing one in such processes that lead toward growth and synthesis. It is in the spirit of inquiry that the Voicework operates, and it allows for great individual variation within an area of personal interrogation. The challenge posed by the Voicework is the ongoing dialogue between the parts of the self that seek reconciliation, and in this it finds a pact with yoga. Thus, while the words in the above citation may not be equivalent to those used in the Voicework, they provide useful areas for deeper probing and reframing. These words evoke their opposites by virtue of yoga being a holistic system and provide a basis for further understanding Voicework theory. Since both systems involve synthesis of dualities, it is possible to look at these concurrent processes in the terms of the oppositions that they both employ.

MEDITATION VERSUS FITZMAURICE VOICEWORK'S DESTRUCTURING PHASE

The concept of observation in the above citation corresponds to the inner awareness engendered through destructuring. The parallel approach to the inner world in yoga is via meditation. Although Fitzmaurice does not use traditional yogic meditation, it is so basic to the understanding of yogic practice that it must be examined to draw a theoretical discourse with the Voicework. In contrasting meditation to destructuring, there are fundamental differences. If those differences are interrogated further, however, some interesting conjunctions emerge. For example, disentanglement or detachment – *pratyahara* – seems diametrically opposed to the commitment to sensuous, messy experience that is incumbent upon an actor engaged in the Voicework. The start point of working "with the sensory stimuli which bombard the mental field" fits with destructuring but the goal is not to "tune out the senses" (Rama, Ballentine, and Ajaya 83). From this, the conclusion may be drawn that detachment is not the means in Fitzmaurice Voicework. Sensory immersion leads to unknown parts of the mind through a similar navigation of images, fantasy and memory, but they are approached with an embracing spirit rather than an avoiding one. This would seem to preclude a connection between destructuring and meditation. Yet, there is isolation in destructuring, as the actor with eyes closed, goes on a personal quest within. In this way there is a kind of sensory withdrawal from the daily routine, and the ordinary external world. This closed inner realm becomes a possible source for creativity. In the publication of a study involving sensory deprivation, one researcher observed, "The emergence of primary process material or regression in the experimental situation can be utilized constructively by the subject...for either problem solving or the achievement of creative synthesis of experience" (Solomon et al. 232). Detachment, also, is not excluded from the creative quest of the Voicework. During and after the work of destructuring, it is possible for an individual to make informed choices that are detached from a previous habitual pattern, although these choices would not be classified as dispassionate.

Also, yoga traditionally seeks transcendence of such human conditions as suffering, desire and fear. This is in opposition to Reich, who basically advanced a philosophy that immersed humanity in the complexity of life trusting to an innate self-regulating mechanism. Iyengar writes, "This is the real meaning of Yoga – a deliverance from contact with pain and sorrow"(Light on Yoga 19). Fitzmaurice Voicework, as many other systems of actor training, does not avoid such human emotions but seeks to allow them to serve as a source or stimulation for creative expression. In fact, destructuring is clearly more of a submersion into the body/mind complex rather than "a deliverance from" it. By contrast, through yogic meditation, *buddhi*, or the higher intuitive mind, separates from *manas*, "the lower mind, which is understood as a relay station for the senses" (Feuerstein 456) on its journey toward synthesis with the Infinite. In the Voicework, a parallel union takes place between lower and higher minds through ANS/CNS synthesis that ignites a creative spark and finds outlet through vocal expression. That creative spark comes from the same source as Reich's orgone energy and, as such, can also be seen as having spiritual as well as sexual potency. This is not unlike the cosmic prana that resides in the human body known as the *kundalini-shakti* that also has dual sexual/spiritual aspects. A common ground, therefore, can be established between these two systems, although the destinations are dissimilar.

At this point, distinctions must be made between sublimation, transmutation and transcendence. If one allows that sublimation can be repressive or expressive in re-channeling energy, then the Voicework prefers a resonance with the expressive sort. Transmutation also is applicable through the Voicework's ability to change habits, patterns, and emotional states to something different. Yet to the extent that the transmutation in the psychophysical matrix shifts the same essential life energy, the alteration is relative. In other words, in transmutation, the manifestation changes but not the underlying essence. This is represented by Reich's functional identity between mind and body. Transmutation, in this sense, has the democratic feel of laterality. Whereas transmutation may occur on a horizontal plane, transcendence always involves the notion of verticality and elevation. It is a change moving upward. The word sublimation derives from sublime and contains the idea of refining, purifying and ennobling and therefore has the connotation of ascent too. This term is applicable to the Voicework through its process of invigorating, clarifying and inspiring the actor's sound that is primed for the heightened realm of theater, whereas transcendence, in a strict theological sense, involves complete separation from the material world through assent and is not applicable to the Voicework. In yoga, transcendence moves one to a state that is unchanging (Feuerstein 77), whereas in the Voicework attendant to the specific demands of acting and human nature, transformation is an on-going process. Thus, in the Voicework the process of change moves in multiple directions to maximize creative freedom without separating the actor from the body or from the emotional state, and yet there is some detachment through informed choice.

In yogic theory, emotional states are the result of a predominance of one of three qualities called *gunas*: *sattvic* (balanced), *rajastic* (excessive), and *tamasic* (deficient) (Kraftsow, <u>Wellness</u> 308). Since health and well-being are cornerstones to the yogic lifestyle, the aim of practice is to attain predominance of emotional balance through the sattvic guna. In actuality, however, these three qualities are in a constant dynamic tension with each other constituting a cycle. Paradoxically, the sattvic attitude is maintained not by striving to keep a harmonic state but by the willingness to observe the loss of it with detachment. In this theory, according to yoga teacher Gary Kraftsow, "The rajo guna can be characterized as an energy of activity and creativity" (<u>Wellness</u> 308). In addition, the dynamic rajastic guna is also responsible for the emotions that characterize fight and flight, such as anger and anxiety that are often unearthed in the Voicework through tremoring. Yoga's approach to these emotions is to "defuse", manage or reduce them (Kraftsow, <u>Wellness</u> 308-9) through breath control and meditation. It is stated in <u>Yoga and Psychotherapy</u>, "The psychophysiological changes produced by meditation seem to be the opposite of those seen in the 'fight and flight' reaction" (Rama, Ballentine, and Ajaya 155). The authors include in the justification for their statement scientifically observed physiological changes that are associated with a feeling of calm such as decreased sweating, more regular breath rate and a switch to theta brain wave activity. "This theta activity would suggest the attainment of a state where reverie and imagery are prominent" (155). Furthermore, Funderburk cites studies that link theta waves with "periods of high creativity" (111). Here lies a testimonial to yoga's paradoxical nature since rajastic activity and its apparent opposite relaxation both lead to creativity. This paradox actually supports the Voicework through the embodiment of the state of relaxed alertness that it moves the actor toward.

Deeper relaxation leads to the delta states of sleep (Funderburk, 113) and this would correspond to the tamasic quality. From this it may be hypothesized that since Fitzmaurice Voicework moves toward creative states, theta waves may also be induced, and this is accomplished not through the controlling technique of meditation as an antidote to the fight/flight emotions but through giving in to the emotional flow when tremoring. Following this yogic construct, in the dynamic system of Voicework, Fitzmaurice instructs the actor to walk a tightrope between rajastic and tamasic possibilities and arrives at the sattvic calm of balance. But it is a balance that is not static as it involves the expression and reception of stimuli. One learns to relax in the active state. In both meditation and Voicework, the purpose is to inhabit a state of relaxed alertness. From here the person can make choices involving separation from the lower self as in yoga or can utilize deep aspects of the lower self in conjunction with the higher self for creativity as in the Voicework.

The conjoining of opposites continues through the discussion of the thematic balance between control and surrender that undergirds both systems of synthesis. In yoga all fears are related to fear of change, and on a primal level that equates to fear of death. Death is seen as part of one's evolution and growth. This idea links to spiritual transformation in yoga through surrender to the inevitable and parallels creative transitions in the Voicework. The Voicework finds philosophical harmony with Krishnamurti when he writes, "As long as we are frightened of life, we shall be frightened of death. The man who is not frightened of life is not frightened of being completely insecure, for he understands that inwardly, psychologically, there is no security. When there is no security there is an endless movement and then life and death are the same" (77). Krishnamurti's "endless movement" points the way to the creative flow that is a goal in the Voicework. Both yoga and Voicework employ the concept of letting go, but the former more often requires separating *from*, while the latter involves letting go *into*. Sometimes, however, in actual practice the borders blur for while the word control is more commonly used in yoga and management is employed in Voicework, there is compatibility in the concept of "passive volition" to counter non-productive effort or straining toward a goal:

> It is only when an attitude of what has been termed 'passive volition'
> is adopted that success is achieved. Passive volition involves an atti-
> tude of letting it happen, of just observing things rather than try-
> ing to gain active control over what is happening. Many students

> working with the control of physiological functioning find that it
> is only when they 'give up' that real change begins to take place
> (Ajaya, Yoga Psychology 42).

Ajaya suggests a 'letting go' of mental expectation and physical tension that connects to Reich's idea of surrender. Expectation and tension are not completely viewed as counter productive in the Voicework, however, since it is through the inducement of longing and physical challenge through the bioenergetically based postures that a tangible relationship to surrender occurs.

In understanding how the Voicework both differs and resembles meditation, there is a significant light thrown upon the Voicework and how it benefits the actor in promoting the creative process. Swami Ajaya in his book, Yoga Psychology gives a detailed description of meditation. He writes, "In meditation there is a definite goal, namely, to experience the highest state of consciousness and to feel greater joy and peace. Allowing the mind to simply drift where it will is contrary to these goals and the process of reaching them" (3). From this it can be argued that meditation is an ordering system while destructuring set on dissolving rigidities appears as a liberating system. Yet, paradoxically, meditation promises spiritual liberation and while destructuring promotes a stream of consciousness mentality through physical tremoring, the imagery, memories and emotions that surface are not seen as haphazard but meaningful in restoring a sense of centeredness and pleasure that conforms with liberated awareness. Admittedly, the physical procedures are different with the meditator usually seated in a fixed pose and the tremorer moving into semi-stressful bioenergetic positions. But it is, in fact, the position and the concentration on specific physical points of awareness that keeps the mind from simply drifting "where it will", for the mind can be called back to a point of focus while tremoring. These observatory points of awareness keep the mind channeled even in the improvisational tremoring mode.

Continuing his description, Swami Ajaya, referring to the ancient sages, notes that:

> By using the tool of introspection, they tried to put the whole com-
> plex puzzle into meaningful order. They watched the way their feel-
> ings and thoughts arose, the way they became interested in certain
> things, what made them miserable and unhappy, and what made
> them feel joyous. They delved deeper and deeper into the subtle

workings of the mind and found that the more they explored, the calmer their minds become. They began to find that through this process they could reach new levels of consciousness.

As they continued self-study, their sensitivity to experiences of body and mind greatly increased. As they learned to sit quietly for long periods of time, they began to observe how thoughts arose in their minds, then led to emotions and finally actions. Through such study of the internal states, these ancient sages began to become aware of the way in which the workings of the mind and the body were controlled. They were then able to alter their mental and physical states at will (Yoga Psychology 4-5).

Both the Voicework and yoga are methods that are conducive for relaxing and tapping into a deep source. As such, both systems bring the aspirant into the present. The destructured actor, in a state of energetic flow, has potentially uncovered the same insights via observation of an inner world and is free to make choices based on greater sensitivity. Such an actor is aligned with the sages in tuning in to the same creative source. Destructuring is in this sense a kind of meditation. Fitzmaurice, however, does not use the term meditation in her teaching, and the connections drawn are informative only to the extent that the actor gleans greater freedom in expression by conceiving of the Voicework as a form of deep self-study. The Voicework does not just involve watching but experiencing the feelings and thoughts that arise, and while calm may be a by-product of such exploration and an asset to creative engagement, it is arrived at not by control but through permission.

As Ajaya goes on to detail the process involved in meditation sharp discrepancies arise with the Voicework:

> The first stage of meditation involves becoming aware of your distracted and chaotic mind. Once you do this, you are able to begin correcting your deficiencies...The process of meditation is similar to that of psychotherapy in that it brings impressions which ordinarily remain in the unconscious to the conscious mind so that they may be brought under scrutiny and may then be controlled. Thus you can decide how realistic a fear or worry or expectation is and dismiss it if you choose. You can decide consciously how to act

instead of reacting blindly on the basis of thoughts which remain buried in your unconscious. Once the thoughts come into your consciousness they no longer carry an impelling driven quality. Those thoughts which are not helpful to you can then be dismissed from your mind entirely. The process of meditation involves first becoming aware of the associative train of thoughts and then learning how to dismiss it instead of becoming carried away by them. As the turbulent thoughts are released, the mind and body are calmed (Yoga Psychology 11).

Immediately there is dissention here in how Fitzmaurice views chaos. Her attitude to inner chaos is that it is neither negative nor equivalent to confusion. In addition, there is no implication of a deficient mind/body split, for in the Voicework, chaos is seen as a creative energy that leads to order. The tremoring body/mind is chaotic toward unity rather than confusion, since chaos contains the energy that heals the split. For Fitzmaurice there are valuable, insightful clues and clarity to be discovered in the so-called vagaries of the mind. This contrasts with Rama, Ballentine, and Ajaya's description of the divided self when they assert "A higher integrating function is missing ... The lower mind, *manas*, when functioning alone can only react mechanically to circumstances or impulses" (80). In the Voicework, those impulses of the lower instinctive self become the treasure trove of creativity and following the recovery scheme of the work, lead to higher functioning without being suppressed by it. There persists a dynamic play between lower and higher selves; between instinct and reason that permit the most sophisticated of communications to contain the boiling energy of chaos within it. Thus, chaos is not eliminated even in the phase of restructuring. In yogic theory, however, there is the goal to eliminate peripheral vision in service of a fixed focus on the infinite. "If his will is unshakable, he can avoid being pulled into involvement with the alluring images in the personal unconscious or into struggles with those which threaten his narrow I-ness. If his attention is focused fixedly on his destination, which lies beyond the personal unconscious, he may be able to successfully traverse it" (Rama, Ballentine, and Ajaya 130). Even in the 'focus-line' of Voicework terminology, there is an important infusion of peripheral, panoramic vision that operates. This differs from the "global witness consciousness" described in Yoga and Psychotherapy, because that awareness is essentially dispassionate (99).

Detachment and distance conjures up Diderot's prescriptions to the actor, but Fitzmaurice, while supporting the objectivity that comes with seeing and the maintenance of mental clarity, doesn't hold that objectivity precludes emotional involvement. Breath is global with awareness in Fitzmaurice Voicework, and there is, through the breath, an activation of sensation that is appropriate for an actor that lives through experience. Both Fitzmaurice Voicework and yoga evoke the same energy–the same vital forces–higher and lower. Both travel toward a destination of acknowledgment and an enlarged sense of self. Both invite energetic and spiritual endeavors with transformative potential. Both isolate the self in order to merge with a deeper self. Both seek to manage or arrange flows of stimuli through letting go. Yet there is a fundamental difference, for in the Voicework, chaos is not antithetical to creative enlightenment. In fact, chaos enriches the actor's clarity of expression, whereas in traditional schools of yoga, there is a choice that must be made to eliminate the chaotic elements; to subdue the disorder or quell the passions.

Because chaos is honored, a more permissive attitude may be inherent to Fitzmaurice Voicework toward the inner world. The approaching attitude seems to be a definitive distinction, and perhaps this is an area where the traditional language of yoga could learn from the more permissive tone of the Voicework. Meditation might be less arduous and resistance to static postures less marked if one adopts an attitude of acceptance of disorder, starting from the open approach of trusting the inner movement of the mind toward calm. But since there are yogis who also take a gentle approach, it is not possible to limit them to one attitude. In The Spirit and Practice of Moving into Stillness, Erich Shiffmann, for example, a yogi who is less judgmental, avows the "self-corrective nature of this transformational discipline" (311) and offers the option of releasing rather than controlling the breath. Shiffmann offers harmonious merger with Voicework theory, where corrections become inner shifts of energy and arrive from contact with the deeper sensitivity predicated on inner listening. He suggests "an underlying spiritual orderliness to all things" (314) that comes from feeling deeply.

Nevertheless, there is a distinction from traditional yoga in the fact that Fitzmaurice Voicework operates from the standpoint of entering the chaos of the mind as a way of clarifying and creating a space for something new rather than emptying the mind. Surrender is a term used in both the Voicework and yoga, but in the latter, it often means letting something go. "Be aware that a thought is floating through your mind, and instead of getting involved with it, simply let it go. Let it bubble up and float away. Be more interested in experiencing the feeling-tone of the arena in which all of this is happening. Orient yourself toward the feeling of peace" (Schiffmann 318). The preference for inner peace does not, however, gel with Fitzmaurice Voicework, and the kind of permission often suggested by yogis is squarely yoked to the cosmos to the exclusion of the mundane, so that there is still an inducement to bring the mind back on track from distractions. For Fitzmaurice, the pursuit of a distraction may offer another road in to greater awareness and more vocal release.

Additionally, the obvious emphasis on silence in meditation is absent in the Voicework, although while tremoring, one appreciates the need for inner listening as a balance to sound release, just as inspiration and expiration create an important parallel. In the Voicework, as the thought comes up, the inducement is to allow it and to let it move and sound through the body. Rather than noticing the thought or sensation peripherally and bringing it back to a center, the new thought, energetic sensation or tremor becomes the center of the moment. The Voicework permits both the letting go of thoughts and the letting go into thoughts. It is not a situation of either/or but of this and that in the Voicework as the actor refines choice making ability. Thus, two roads lead to the inner clarification: the yogic one of mental relaxation and the one of following impulses and mental images. Ultimately, however, both systems lead to the flow that Schiffmann describes:

> Then, during the day, do and be as the energy – *your* energy – is
> prompting you to do or be. Move with the flow. Or rather, you are
> the flow, and if you simply let yourself be in the now – not know-
> ing how you are supposed to be – the flow will move through you
> unimpeded, without preconception, and it will be very clear to you
> how you should be and how you should respond. The energy will
> move you. You will be inspired to action. It will feel like you are
> running on free energy (327).

While meditation may have some very deep connections to the Fitzmaurice Voicework destructuring phase, the conclusion shows that they should not be equated. For while the actor enters a dark world in tremoring and is mindful of inner visions, there is no need to detach from the feelings that those images evoke. Detachment in the Voicework always ideally accompanies informed choice that needn't preclude emotional vitality. The actor is encouraged to experience rather than control or transcend thoughts and emotions that arise. In yoga and the Voicework, it is through the contact with the inner world that the higher parts of the self are recovered. In the Voicework, however, the so-called lower self is never actually transcended in a theological sense, though it may be transmuted and sublimated. This lower self infuses the awareness of the higher functions when the actor communicates articulately and intelligently without losing deep, primal energies. Meditation is typically silent, and while meditation may be done with chants or mantras, these tend to be predetermined, organized sounds and contrapose very sharply with the fluffy sound and impulsive releases that accompany tremoring. In addition, because of its sensuous nature, the Voicework privileges feeling the sound rather than listening as might occur when reciting a mantra. Then there is the important element of the performance and vocal expression that becomes the destination for the disciplines of the class, rather than the privileging of non-exhibitory practice and silence that are the goals of the ashram. The distinctions between the two in the attitude, the physical process, and the overt foregrounding or not of a spiritual goal continue in the channeling, "controlling" or what Fitzmaurice calls the managing phase.

PRANAYAMA VERSUS THE THEORY OF BREATH IN FITZMAURICE VOICEWORK

The managing, or restructured breathing phase parallels the pranayama techniques of yoga with significant distinctions. B.K.S. Iyengar gives a definition:

Prana means breath, respiration, life, vitality, wind, energy or strength. It also connotes the soul as opposed to the body. The word is generally used in the plural to indicate vital breaths. Ayama means length, expansion, stretching or restraint. Pranayama thus connotes extension of breath and its control. This extension is over all the functions of breathing, namely, (1) inhalation or inspiration, which is termed puraka (filling up); (2) exhalation or expiration, which is called rechaka (emptying the lungs), and (3) retention or holding the breath, a state where there is no inhalation or exhalation, which is termed kumbhaka...Similarly, there are two states of kumbhaka namely (1) when breathing is suspended after full inhalation (the lungs being completely filled with life-giving air), and (2) when breathing is suspended after full exhalation (the lungs being emptied of all noxious air) (Light on Yoga 43).

85

The goal of pranayama is to prepare one for meditation. Most pranayama techniques involve nostril breathing. A big distinction with the Voicework, of course, because it involves voice and speech, requires that the actor breathe through the mouth rather than the nose exclusively. And while the concept of "the prolongation of breath and its restraint" (Iyengar, Light on Pranayama 13) parallels the Voicework's management of breath in the restructuring phase, the focus is less on holding the breath back and more on not permitting collapse of the respiratory organization.

In yoga metaphysics, nostril breathing mirrors the sun/moon connotation of hatha yoga with solar energy traveling through the passageway of the right nostril and lunar energy coursing through the left. The right channel, or *nadi,* is called *pingala* and the left is called *ida.* These *nadis* run vertically bilaterally to the center channel called susumna that runs through the center of the spine. The right and left nostril's airflow energetic is heating and cooling respectively. By learning to regulate the flow of air through these channels, the yogi alters physical and mental states (Kraftsow, Yoga for Transformation 125-6). The authors of Yoga and Psychotherapy make a scientific connection with the hemispheres of the brain, so that the solar right nostril relates to the left side of the brain, and its dominance is most evident in assertive activities, while the lunar left nostril's openness is more suited to tasks where receptivity is more the requirement (Rama, Ballentine and Ajaya 41). Through this cerebral connection, right/left nostril breathing regulates sympathetic and parasympathetic nervous system activities respectively (Feuerstein 353).

If the Voicework follows this logic, then the actor, via tremoring and restructuring, self-regulates the degree of openness in each nostril depending on the task or situation at hand. The actor is prepared, through a variety of encounters with mental and emotional stimuli in destructuring, to experience a number of scenarios that permit both activity and reactivity. When successful, these experiences prime the whole body/mind complex to coordinate breath when it is involved in structuring situations. In training, these structured breath coordinations must be conscious, involving the transverses and intercostal muscles. With repetition they become automatic and synchronized so the actor can operate with full immersion in the situation, while simultaneously maintaining precision concerning the breath support process.

Purification is another goal in pranayama. "The respiratory system is the gateway to purifying the body, mind and intellect. The key to this is pranayama" (Iyengar, Light on Pranayama, 17). Physical, mental and emotional toxins are released in the Voicework as well, since bioenergetics on which it is built is a healing modality that provides for internal cleansing through breathing. In step with yoga, the Voicework also adheres to the primacy of the breath. Iyengar concurs that breath is of principle importance:

> The Kuasitaki Upanisad says 'One can live deprived of speech, for we see the dumb; one deprived of sight, for we see the blind; of hearing, for we see the deaf; and of mind, for we see the childish; one can live without arms and legs, for thus we see. But now it is the breathing spirit alone, the intelligence-self that seizes hold of this body and makes it rise up. This is the all obtaining in the breathing spirit. What is the breathing spirit, that is the intelligence-self. What is intelligence-self, that is the breathing spirit, for together they live in this body and together they go out of it'" (Light on Pranayama 19).

In a more mundane way, Virgil Anderson supports this observation in Training the Speaking Voice by identifying speech as an overlaid function, indicating that the organs used for speaking have primary purposes that supersede vocal expression (56). In this way, he points the way to the need for assuring that vocal and speech education do not interfere with the more basic survival activities of the organism. Thus a voice training system needs to honor the primary nature of breath to have lasting effectiveness. This concept marries well with the Voicework's destructuring phase where the unearthing of primal, innate impulses informs the breath, and fluffy sound releases and extends to the restructuring phase when the actor is required to maintain those original links while transiting into conscious speech.

Both *Cit* and *Citta* or *Chitta* are Sanskrit words for consciousness. They are distinguished by Georg Feuerstein when he defines *Cit* as " Pure awareness, or the transcendental Consciousness beyond all thought; the eternal witness" and *Citta* as the "The finite mind, psyche, or consciousness, which is dependent on the play of attention, as opposed to *cit* (454). Iyengar further illuminates consciousness by describing mind, desire and breath in a dynamic interplay:

> Chitta and prana are in constant association. Where there is chitta there prana is focused, and where prana is there chitta is focused. The chitta is like a vehicle propelled by two powerful forces, prana and vasana (desires). It moves in the direction of the more powerful force. As a ball rebounds when struck to the ground, so is the

sadhaka *(aspirant)* tossed according to the movement of prana and chitta. If breath (prana) prevails, then the desires are controlled, the senses are held in check and the mind is stilled. If the force of desire prevails, the breathing becomes uneven and the mind gets agitated (<u>Light on Pranayama</u> 13).

In Fitzmaurice Voicework, the arrow can travel both ways productively, depending upon the desired outcomes. In a way, desire taking over the body and breath parallels the agitation of destructuring. But it must be remembered that the agitation of the tremor is consciously induced, and the vocal energy released is ultimately manageable in the restructuring phase. Then, in restructuring, prana/breath learns to harness vasana/desire for creative tasks that engender a centered mind and body consciousness. What Iyengar describes as a tossed agitated movement compares both to the tremor and to the state that the tremor seeks to heal. This refers back to the distinction Fitzmaurice makes between spasm and tremor. Agitation may be destructive if there is rigidity or a denial of expressiveness according to Voicework theory. The same agitation, however, may be an invitation to resolution and liberation if the energy is engaged constructively through tremoring. Ideally, the tremoring process brings the agitated mind to clarity through motion and sound with breath fueling both.

In this way, the breath equates with inspiration in the sense of uplifting, creative thinking. In <u>Science of Breath</u>, Rama, Ballentine and Hymes assert that breath/prana/energy is the intermediate level between body and mind, and in order for the body to affect mind or vice-versa, the agency of altering the breath is necessary. "Prana is the life-force, vital energy and "breath is the vehicle for prana" (8). They go on to note: "When someone feels more energy, more mental energy and creativity, we say of him that he has become 'inspired'; there is an 'inspiration'. We indicate through our language an intuitive recognition of the relationship between the breath and the vital energy, its necessity for life and its necessity for creativity" (<u>Science</u> 9). Instinct connects to intuition via inspiration in the Voicework through the conjunction of autonomic and central nervous systems. It is not these separate systems that permit the entry of intuition, but their synthesis. Intuition comes through reception as the Voicework sets up experimental body configurations, some resembling asanas that provide a fertile ground for self-exploration and release. By utilizing the breath as a gauge and a key for this inner journey, the actor discovers new modes of communication; some occurring intuitively.   Support for such discovery can be found in <u>Science of Breath</u>:

> ...for if it is true that breath influences both body and mind, then the rhythm and the rate of the breath would reflect not only one's physical condition, but it would also help to create it. It would in addition be an indication of one's emotional and mental state as well as an influence on, and a help in creating, that state. Therefore, what is going on in the totality of a person could be judged from his breathing" (9).

Thus, an argument resonating with the Voicework is made that character can be assessed via how the person breathes.

Fitzmaurice Voicework utilizes this information in order to read the character patterns of the actor and provide the possibility of breathing shifts through destructuring that offer support for alteration, if needed for fuller expression.   In yoga the word prana can be used for breath or energy interchangeably. As a master teacher, Fitzmaurice has acquired the ability to read energy patterns that fits with Rama, Ballentine and Hymes description when they state, "Energy is being consumed in one place and produced or stored up in another. It is being shifted from this point to that, resulting in a net movement of energy so that we might say there is an energy 'flow,' and if we could stand back and look at this continually shifting picture, we would be able to map out an overall pattern of flux" (10). This seeing of energy parallels Reichian therapy's and Lowen's bioenergetic body/breath observations. The common ground of visual assessment reifies even more exactly in Pierrakos' <u>Core Energetics</u>, where he incorporates aura reading that is based in the yoga tradition. Fitzmaurice Voicework integrates aspects of both pranic (breath/energy) reading and bioenergetic physical assessment. Through her work with Pierrakos and Barbara Brennan, a research physicist turned healer, she extends to aura reading too.

Breath itself is a restructuring force that creates patterns of energy. "With each breath energy flows through the body in waves, and this flow of breath is constantly shaping and restructuring that pattern of energy which comprises the *pranic* body" (Rama, Ballentine, and Hymes 12). Here, in yoga, is a new suggestion that the breath itself is a trigger for shape shifting that is also reflected in the destructuring phase–the exploratory phase of the Voicework. The body is thus subject to the energy flow that forms and reshapes it:

If we look at physiology from this point of view we begin to realize that the material body (which we have tended up to this time to regard as primary) is, in fact, secondary. Its existence is based on something more fundamental than itself. The flow of energy creates and sustains the tissues of the body, and if the energy pattern is sufficiently changed then the physical body will change. If the energy pattern is altered drastically enough the body can be completely transformed, either for better or worse (Rama, Ballentine, Hymes 12).

The authors conclude: "The physical body is nothing more than a crystallization around the energy pattern that underlies it" (13). It is these subterranean energy patters that Fitzmaurice Voicework seeks to unearth. But the authors' conclusion need not demote the importance of the physical body since the manifestation of energy depends upon pranic and corporeal vehicles that carry it. In Fitzmaurice Voicework, as in the theory put forth in this book, there is a permeable exchange between body, breath, mind and desire–all energetic aspects of each other, all entrance points to creativity.

One practices mindful breathing so that when under stress in less pedagogically driven situations, there is a new reflexive habit that has been built up. In this way, while the technical procedures of pranayama are at odds with the chaotic destructured breathing and restructured managed breath, the template towards transformation is the same. Both train the person to greater choice making and mastery beyond the ashram or the classroom. Fitzmaurice would question the assertion that unconscious breathing is innately haphazard (Rama, Ballentine, and Hymes 19) and would make a distinction between the culturally induced restrictive breathing habits that become unconscious from those unconsciously buried ones that are deeply primal and natural to the organism's survival instincts. While these yogis are saying detach from this "haphazard" effort and go deep, Fitzmaurice is suggesting that one go into the haphazardness to reach the depth. This primal mode of breathing contains valuable insights and rich creative food for expression that constitutes recovery of lost wisdom, which deepens the actor's resources for communication. Yoga also recognizes the primal importance of breath in another aspect:

> The breath begins at a strategic point in development. The first great adaptation to the outside world made by the newborn is his initial

gasp for air. The beginning of respiration transforms the dynamics of the circulatory system and gears the infant's physiology to its new environment. Nothing so arouses primitive survival instincts as does the feeling of suffocation. For this reason, the flow of breath and its alterations and rhythms is intimately tied in with the earliest, most fundamental layers of mental life (Rama, Ballentine, and Ajaya 33).

In the Voicework, one trains consciously so that a balanced responsiveness between choice and unpredictability becomes automatic. It is in order to reconstitute an automatic response system that Fitzmaurice Voicework seeks to stimulate the fight/flight mechanism. In the relative safety of the classroom, the actor is guided to interrogate and deconstruct patterns of bracing; to surrender the unconsciously culture-driven role; to resurrect the alternative spontaneous reflexes of the autonomic nervous system. Because this is consciously undertaken, the actor then can make shifts in reprogramming the body/mind system toward more supportive creative possibilities. A connection is made to consciousness and the autonomic nervous system through pranayama that is different:

> Patanjali, the codifier of yoga science, explains that the control of *prana* is the regulation of inhalation and exhalation. This is accomplished by eliminating the pause between inhalation and exhalation or expanding it by retention. Then, by regulating the motion of the lungs, the heart and the vagus nerve are controlled...The science of pranayama is thus intimately connected with the autonomic nervous system and brings its functions under conscious control through the functioning of the lungs. Here is a unique exception to the rule that the autonomic nervous system governs processes that are self-regulating and not under voluntary control. Though the act of respiration is for the most part involuntary, voluntary control in this area is easily achieved, for the depth, duration and frequency of respiration can be consciously modulated quite readily. It is for this reason that control of breath constitutes an obvious starting point toward attainment of control over the functioning of the autonomic nervous system (Rama, Ballentine, and Hymes 95).

Here an important distinction must be made. The Voicework is not seeking to bring the breath under conscious control as much as it is involved in allowing an undisciplined chaotic breath to determine structure based on the communicative needs of the person. For example, unlike pranayama, Fitzmaurice Voicework does not advocate the forced, controlled exhalations of *ujjayi* breathing. According to the authors of Science of Breath:

> Inhalation and exhalation during *ujjayi* are slow and deep, and take place with partial closure of the glottis. This produces a sound like sobbing, but it is even and continuous. During inhalation the incoming air is felt on the roof of the palate and is accompanied by the sibilant sound *sa*. During exhalation the outgoing air is felt on the roof of the palate and is accompanied by the aspirate sound *ha*. During inhalation the abdominal muscles are kept slightly contracted, and during exhalation abdominal pressure is exerted till the breath is completely expelled (Rama, Ballentine, and Hymes 119).

In the Voicework, by arousing fight and flight mechanisms, the idea is to let the breath move globally through the body to transform emotion into creative power. Emotional energy manifests palpably as pockets of tension in the anatomy. Reich mentions segments of the body where energy flow is blocked: the eyes, mouth, neck, chest, diaphragm, abdomen and pelvis. All of these areas are important in assisting the person to dismantle tension.

Both Voicework teachers and yogis discuss the chest as residence of the lungs. It is important, often with the guidance of a teacher, not to get stuck in the chest for the reason outlined in Science of Breath:

> Though chest breathing has now become natural and involuntary for most of us, it is really a part of the fight/flight syndrome, aroused when the organism is challenged by some external stress or danger. Because of the reciprocity between breath and mind, chest breathing, in turn, gives rise to the tension and anxiety associated with the fight/flight syndrome. With chest breathing, the breath is shallow, jerky and unsteady, resulting in similar unsteadiness of the mind. All techniques aimed at providing relaxation of the body, nerves and mind will be ineffective unless chest breathing is

replaced by deep, even and steady diaphragmatic breathing (Rama, Ballentine, and Hymes 109).

One may ask why evoke a response that is essentially seen as inefficient or tension producing. It must be clarified, however, that in the spirit of deep self-study, the Voicework seeks to provide an opportunity of learning for the actor to understand the origin of both the habits that cause anxiety and the innate power of choice that may be used to alter them. Fight and flight reactions, when aroused in this way, become a learning tool that reinforces the need for more efficacious habits through an experience that is visceral and not merely intellectual. Also, because fight/flight breathing is a heightened breath, Fitzmaurice Voicework utilizes it by transferring it away from destructive habits to creative ones such as performance. Iyengar recognizes this high voltage content to prana when he writes, "All vibrating energies are prana. All physical energies such as heat, light, gravity, magnetism and electricity are also prana. It is hidden or potential energy in all beings released to the fullest extent in times of danger" (Light on Pranayama 12). Those times of danger evoked in the experimental setting of the classroom, permit the liberation of potent charged energy through the breath that Fitzmaurice asks the actor to engage with in order to self-correct and to harness for vocal authenticity.

The breath in the Voicework, as in yoga, is only a means to an end in transforming body and mind. Funderburk's reinforcement of this goal for yoga also applies to the Voicework when he clarifies that pranayama is not designed to control the breath patterns but "pranic or energy patterns" (47). Therefore, management of the breath is a means to an end that aligns the yogic goal of calm and centeredness with the Voicework's one of creative fulfillment. While spirit may not be privileged as it is in religious pursuits, the nature of the breath is so semantically charged that there is an implicit spiritual undercurrent in the Voicework as well. We are reminded that "the fundamental relationship between breath and 'spirit' is reflected in most languages, viz: our 'expiration' and 'inspiration,' the latter meaning not only to *inhale*, but to become filled with creative energy or spirit (inspired). The word 'expiration' denotes death, or loss of life-energy as well as 'exhalation'" (Rama, Ballentine, and Ajaya 33). Fitzmaurice supports the spiritual underpinning of the meaning of breath when she writes: "Inspiration denotes both an inhalation and a creative idea. Breathing is meaning. And respiration is identified with spirit, coming from the same Latin root" ("Zeami Breathing" 201).

Before leaving the discussion of yogic breathing in relation to the Voicework, a point must be made about sequencing. Since pranayama is a preparation to meditation, sequentially there is a turnabout with Voicework if an analogy is made pairing restructuring with pranayama. In yoga books, the sequencing is usually asana, pranayama and then meditation. In FV the movement is from the most internal to the more external; from the inner world to the performance.

ASANAS AND FITZMAURICE VOICEWORK POSTURES

The most apparent intersection with Voicework and yoga occurs in the asanas, or yogic postures. In defining asana, the renowned yoga teacher, T.K. V. Desikachar notes: "The word is derived from the Sanskrit root as which means 'to stay,' 'to be,' 'to sit,' or to be established in a particular position" (17). Iyengar distinguishes yoga asanas from other physical culture in their aim to train the mind not just the body (Light on Yoga 40-1). Mere attention to external performance of the asanas reduces them to calisthenics. This philosophy also underscores Fitzmaurice positions that offer a physical terrain in which to encounter, receive, explore and integrate mental processes. For in training the voice, one is also training the mind. While not advocating the self-mortification that in the West has traditionally been associated with yogis and that provides the grounds for Reich's disapproval of asceticism, Iyengar is not prescribing the denial of the body but views it as a path toward the inner life of the mind and spirit. "The yogi conquers the body by the practice of asanas and makes it a fit vehicle for the spirit. He knows that it is a necessary vehicle for the spirit. A soul without a body is like a bird deprived of its power to fly" (Light on Yoga 41). Inspiration and creative spark harmonize with spirit, but the word conquer has militaristic connotations that conflict with the more permissive, democratic approach that the Voicework takes regarding the body. It should be noted, however, that there are different styles and schools of yoga and some of them, such as yin and therapeutic yoga, tend to eliminate such adversarial terminology. Perhaps, the concept of conquering the body should not be taken too literally. The American hatha yoga master, Joel Kramer, presents a philosophical approach to the body that is in complete agreement with Fitzmaurice Voicework:

> The body's resistance should be respected, since it is useful feed-
> back. Trying to conquer resistance and push past pain is actu-
> ally another form of resistance – resistance to your own limits, to

94

what and where you are now. When you change your focus from 'resisting resistance' to channeling energy into where the limits lie, your body can follow its own flow and open on its own, with minimal resistance. Trying forcibly to push past your limits actually creates more resistance and tension, whereas surrendering to the posture ultimately draws you into far greater depth. The body will tell you when to move and deepen if you listen to it ("Yoga as Self-Transformation" 2).

The desire to break down resistance is a mental agenda that is imposed on the body. Such agendas should be interrogated carefully with respect to physical messages. Pain, of course, is an excellent gauge in determining when to aggress and when to surrender in both yoga and Voicework.

Yoga and Fitzmaurice Voicework listen to the characteristics of pain when it occurs in all of its variety in making assessments involving choices for levels of engagement. Pain in either system should not lead to injury. Kramer makes a distinction between pain and intensity:

> The line between them might sometimes appear nebulous, but it is actually well defined by the state of your mind. Pain is not only physical, but psychological, too, for it involves a judgment of discomfort – not liking to be there. If you are running from the feeling, it's pain. Intensity that is not pain generates an energy and sensuous quality that turns you on ("Self-Transformation" 5).

In yoga, the idea is to avoid pain and suffering, but this is at odds with the Voicework and the creative use of the human condition that it elicits through destructuring. Pain is seen here as a necessary component of life and should no more be avoided than pleasure. In the Voicework, actors learn to know their pain and the feelings that accompany it rather than run from them. The Voicework does not exclude playing with varying degrees of intensity in approaching the mind and body, nor does it seek to completely eliminate pain. Rather it asks the actor to trust the wisdom of self-correcting mechanisms in exploring the fight and flight arousal system. Again, this does not mean the need for physical injury nor psychic damage and may initially require the assistance of a skilled teacher to guide the student in making distinctions. Particularly, in encounter with pain, there is the need for opening the breath, permission for relaxation and knowing when not to push past limits, since that could harm the voice and abolish the subtlety of expressiveness. Where the yoga and Voicework systems harmonize is in the sensitized inner listening when painful physical or mental messages arise. The Voicework is not masochistically evoking pain, but when it does occur, the actor is taught to enter it as a learning tool towards greater mind/body integration, and a balance must be had between entering and exiting based on inner listening.

Sensitized listening, however, does not always require non-action. Another category of mental conditioning or resistance can be encountered where the mind is actually repressing the body and its storehouse of emotional information. The nature of thought and mental attitude are vitally important to successful productive sessions in yoga and Voicework. "In fact, most of the real limits that you confront in yoga live in the mind, not the body...I have found it is usually not the body that tires first, but rather, the mind which loses the stamina required for attention" (Kramer, "Self-Transformation" 2). Such mental resistances may have an origin in traumatic memories or restricting self-images. Through destructuring and in yoga asanas, mental limitations are faced, and a respectful approach is still advantageous that honors the wisdom of these protective survival mechanisms. In yoga and Voicework, such inquiry is carried out in the spirit of curiosity and a passionate quest for self-knowledge.

Dual desires, the current and the historical, interlock in a crucible of self discovery that supersede the technical facility of the postures or the ego comforting accomplishment of a satisfactory external appearance. Students who do yoga or others who have strong physical training in dance may already be flexible, and for them the challenge still exists in locating their true inner growth points in the Voicework postures. Finding the tremor is symbolic for this growth point, and Kramer underscores an idea that applies to the Voicework when he notes, "there is also an interplay between transformation and resistance to change. There's no way to remain the way you are now: you either become rigid and crystallized, or you break out of patterns and transform ("Self-Transformation" 2). In those genetically endowed with flexible joints or those who have trained the body to a high degree of elasticity, part of the challenge is to not be seduced by outward mobility but to seek further for inner growth.

Degree of flexibility, as well as chronological age, are not limiting factors in yoga or in the Voicework since both systems are predicated on the notion that people share a human inner psychic architecture that is pliable. Self-images can crumble, and new ones can be resurrected. Lost memories can be recovered and serve as catalysts for growth. Kramer's appreciation of memory parallels the Voicework perspective in its transformative potential, "Memory lives in the cells, in the systems of the body, in the brain, and in thought itself. The paradox of experience is that it both teaches you and limits you. It expands your horizons, and is the ground or matrix from which transformation can occur" ("Self-Transformation" 3). Memory retrieval links with the recovery aspect of both Voicework and yoga. Both systems have therapeutic underpinnings and provide tools for healing. The practice of yoga, through meditation, pranayama and asana, has documented scientific studies showing beneficial health effects. Since there are many areas of overlap theoretically between yoga and Fitzmaurice Voicework, future studies undertaken might prove similar health inducing results, particularly where both systems intersect in their programs toward deep relaxation. But such studies are lacking. Regardless of the Voicework's lack of scientific data confirming its therapeutic worth, Kramer offers a yogi's viewpoint that would be shared by Fitzmaurice in regarding her approach when he states, "The search for a fountain of youth, whether through magic, drugs, or techniques, indicates a resistance to the aging process. I prefer to call yoga a 'fountain of life.' Aging is inevitable. Yoga allows you to approach it awarely as a transformative process that can bring growth and new depths with maturation" ("Self-Transformation 3). Kramer's advice that is reflected in the Voicework allows age to be no discriminating barrier for transformative creativity. This provides a refreshing alternative in a theatrical culture so focused on chronological youth.

Alternative perspectives emanate from the asanas themselves and carry over to the Voicework's tremor positions. Originally, asanas were exclusively sitting postures for meditation. Only later were they expanded to include the variety of positions that comprise hatha yoga. The asanas developed from observation of nature and indicate a high regard for life in both animate and inanimate forms as noted by Iyengar, "Whilst performing asanas the yogi's body assumes many forms resembling a variety of creatures. His mind is trained not to despise any creature, for he knows that throughout the whole gamut of creation, from the lowliest insect to the most perfect sage, there breathes the same Universal Spirit, which assumes innumerable forms" (Light on Yoga 42). This acceptance is in line with the actor's receptivity to character variations, and the Voicework subtly invites such connections through the alteration of the body from conditioned holding patterns to various destructuring, yoga-like postures such as the cobra, the dog, the camel etc.

All asanas are characterized by two required qualities as set forth by Pantanjali, the yoga scholar who recorded them. These goals are alertness and comfort (Desikachar 17). Fitzmaurice Voicework aims for relaxed alertness in all the positions but the achievement of this state may involve periods of discomfort as old habits are jostled from the body, and rigid perceptions are encountered in the mind. Ultimately, there is an ease with relating to one's self in both systems only after honest physical and mental assessment that are personal to the student's developmental rate. Funderburk's argument that the etymological derivation of exercise, meaning "to drive forth (a tillage beast) and hence 'to employ, to set to work'" (3), is in complete antithesis to the asanas because the idea of exercise involves "exertion...vigorous action, effort". This formal distinction breaks down in practice when regarding certain forms of yoga such as yogi Bajhan's kundalini or the more contemporary Bikram. What Funderburk wants to separate, however, is the psycho-spiritual techniques of yoga from the muscle driven activities of the gymnasium. In another sense exercise resonates with exorcise. While one may argue that yoga moves one to union with spirit rather than expulsion, nevertheless, one aim is to drive out negative thoughts and energies. While the Voicework is not exercise in the sense of gymnasium drills, certain aspects of it, particularly the bioenergetically based "hitting the mat" or "tantrum on the mat" could be seen as exercise in the sense of "vigorous action" and the driving out of spirits. The yoga teacher, Doug Keller, however, highlights the vigor involved in asana but ultimately concludes with the importance of remembering the sun/moon theme of balance inherent in yoga practice. "The union is *dynamic*; as a single word, 'hatha' means 'to strike' or 'to force.' It's often assumed that the dominating force in the practice of yoga is willpower. But the power at work in an asana is something far beyond your own individual will. Willpower has to be tempered with surrender if you're to discover the true power of a pose" (104). In the Voicework, the blended convergence couples surrender to creative chaos with clarity of intention as one transitions from destructuring to restructuring. The destructuring positions require, therefore, receptive alertness, focused relaxation, and willful surrender, while the restructuring phase demands the same qualities within the framework of communication.

Furthermore, yoga asanas, like Voicework positions, can be used diagnostically to locate and release tension:

> The various asanas are actually very precise tools. Each yoga
> posture, or asana – pronounced AAH-suh-nuh – is a specific

shape or template in which the stretching occurs. The idea is to use these tools or shapes to help create more space in your body. Your body is the visible and tangible portion of your energy field, and each pose is like a map into a specific area of that field. You create more space by undoing the tight spots, releasing tensions. Therefore, a large part of the practice is about deliberately roving through your body looking for the contracted, painful areas. Using the various poses as maps into yourself, or places to look, you then endeavor to stretch, open, and release the contracted areas. This is extremely pleasurable once you get a feeling for it (Schiffmann 38).

Schiffmann views yoga asanas as a mode of self-research that concurs with the spirit of the Voicework. In both systems the emphasis on inner focus takes the pressure off the student of conforming to external appearance for its own sake. Even when precise instructions are given concerning the details of the exterior shaping, the purpose is to highlight an inner understanding that is best arrived at through the clarity of external technique. Technique, in both systems, is seen as a means to an end, and the determination of method evolves from experimentation that seeks the most effective ways to clear tensions and allow the insights that come with inner observation. Paradoxically, the "means to the end" approach is most effective when the student in both systems is grounded in the present. Thus, Shiffmann notes that the asanas are not "destinations" (45) as much as they are immersions into one's self. In Voicework, tremoring can conjure up a panorama of imagery that spans from past to future, memory to fantasy. To the extent, however, that the experience is tangible, the postures bring the person into the present.

Yoga phraseology can be useful in illuminating Voicework principles as well. Joel Kramer, one of Erich Shiffmann's teachers, presents the concept of "stretching in the nerves" that is additional to muscle and tendon stretch when he clarifies that, "Ordinarily, when we're stretching, we're reaching for an elongation in the musculature. But there's another kind of stretching, that doesn't require great extension or flexibility. It involves using the muscles to move through the nervous system, actually channeling energy in a certain direction through the body ("Mind in Asana" 22). This idea of neural stretching elicits a parallel to the autonomic nervous system and is also applicable in the Voicework positions. Nerve stretching creates what Kramer calls "lines of energy" that suggest a blending of directing the mind via intention and visualization with physical sensation:

> For example, you can create an internal line of energy by holding your arm parallel to the floor and stretching it outward. This brings a vibration that moves from the shoulder out the arm, through the fingers. Each posture has its own lines of energy which can be created at different stages in the posture, and which complement one another and work together to involve the body as a whole ("Self-Transformation" 6).

This concept also occurs in Fitzmaurice Voicework positions that are held and create a physiological dance between control and surrender resulting in the tremor. Schiffmann supports this theory when he instructs, "The muscles of the arm and hand should be taut enough to be on the verge of a slight tremor" (67). In Voicework, as in yoga, the intensity of the line of energy can be varied depending on the degree of physical push or mental channeling. Deepening the breath in the region of stretch fuels the direction of thought. In the same way, it energizes the tremor in the Voicework positions. But there are also moments in a destructuring session where too much mental direction obscures the natural chaos, which textures the flow that contributes valuable information and serves as food for creative impulse. While breath is a constant, the degree of mental and physical activation is a moment-by-moment investigation in destructuring, as it is in yoga.

Another phrase coined by Kramer that finds ideological harmony in the Voicework is "playing edges". The edge is that moment of intensity just short of pain and to play here means to learn, permit and not push:

> Playing edges slowly in this fashion has the advantage of giving you better alignment throughout the whole process, and a sharper capacity to listen to feedback, which enables you to enjoy greater levels of intensity without pain, and minimizes the possibility of injury. Edge playing also allows you to get in touch with the sensual nature of the posture and the quality of feeling in the stretch, so that each pose can become an aesthetic experience ("Self-Transformation" 5).

The edge in the Voicework is an extraordinarily rich borderland of psychosomatic phenomena that is always approached with respect. But the playing of edges may actually induce a desire to launch into further self-discovery. Even when playing beyond the edges, Fitzmaurice Voicework cultivates a sense of inner listening and timing that prohibits violation. Erich Shiffmann details three kinds of edges: the flexibility edge that characterizes how far one can go physically; the endurance edge that has to do with the limit of one's stamina; and the attention edge that proscribes the limit of one's mental focus (74). In identifying the kinds of edges, Shiffmann offers a useful guide to the yogi as well as the Voicework student for the possibility that such edge playing always grounds one in the present. Playing the edge is a tool for increasing awareness and sensitivity in the moment and as such proves useful to the actor. These three edges are subject to degree, which Kramer and Schiffmann call minimum and maximum edge. These edges define the inner journey:

> Most of us are aware of the maximum edge; it is the easiest to
> detect. This is the point where the stretch begins to hurt. It is the
> furthest point of tightness beyond which you should not go. If you
> were to force yourself beyond this point, you would definitely be
> in pain and might easily hurt yourself or pull a muscle...The mini-
> mum edge is where you sense the very first sensation of stretch, the
> very first hint of resistance coming from your muscles (Spirit 78).

Because the focus as outlined by Schiffmann is on the execution of the stretch, there is a fundamental difference with the Voicework, where the direction is not always toward extension but is on the releasing potency of the tremor. This involves an emphasis on developing emotional, imaginative, as well as physical resources for vocal expression. The tools of knowing one's minimum and maximum boundaries still apply, as does the idea of melting rather than forcing those barriers in the journey to the interior, but yoga's mission of inner peace may be at odds with the fight/flight response elicited through tremoring. As Shiffmann notes, "Yoga is not about fighting" (81). His advice is nonetheless ultimately congruent with the Voicework, since he is referring to fighting oneself by forcing postures. Such self-flagellation corresponds to Reich's description of masochism and is not coherent with the Voicework either. In the Voicework, the arousal of the fight and flight reflex is not an end in itself but moves the performer toward exploring edges that inform actions. There remains intact, however, inner sensitivity and reactions that create conscious choices that challenge but don't violate the sanctity of the self.

Fitzmaurice Voicework makes no negative judgment call on the spirit of competition, since achieving objectives is common terminology to both the art and business of acting. Recalling Lowen's positive take on aggression as forward movement, such steps may be therapeutic and appropriate in releasing tension and reaching an inner synthesis for repressed bodies and minds. Nonetheless, Fitzmaurice would agree with the yogi, Joel Kramer, when he states, "If your mind is primarily on the goal, the gap between where you are and where you want to be, can bring tension and hinder movement. You push too hard and fast instead of allowing your body to open at its own pace" ("Self-Transformation" 1). The gap between presence and projection relates directly to the voice in the sense of straining or throwing one's voice out in violation of the body. Both Kramer and Fitzmaurice are suggesting an elegant alternative involving permission within action; an inner attentiveness that grounds one in trusting the present. In the Voicework, gaps are also seen as entrance points and can be the beginning of the inner journey. Disjunctions are physical and emotional spaces that require both interrogation and immersion. Gaps are also outlets and in tremoring can provide space for energy flow that is seeking body/mind unions and insights. Gaps provide borderlands– points where change and resistance to change abut–prompting inner exploration in how one transitions between aggression and surrender. Kramer's view of the dichotomy resonates with the Voicework:

> Yoga involves a balance between 'control' and 'surrender' – between pushing and relaxing, channeling energy and letting go, so the energy can move you. I have found there are basically two personality types in yoga. I call them the 'pushers' and the 'sensualists.' The pushers are more into control and progress – the sensualists into surrender and relaxation. As yoga truly means balance, if your tendency is to push, you must also learn to let go, relax, and enjoy the sensuality of the stretch. If your tendency is to relax, and be 'laid back,' you must learn to experience the turn on of pushing your edges and using control to generate energy ("Self-Transformation" 2).

In the Voicework, such personality gaps are schisms where the body/mind can shift toward altering tremors that lead the way to transformation. Gaps provide fruitful areas of rebellious energy where a variety of inner characters can interact in tremoring dialogue. The mending of gaps is often achieved through the breath. Awareness of the breath is a way to bring the mind into the present in all phases of yoga including meditation and asana. Similarly breath is the way to be present for the destructuring and restructuring actor.

In yoga and Voicework, therefore, it is breath that "animates the stretches" (Schiffmann 39) and gives energetic fluidity. Flow results not from the conscious decision to appear graceful but interweaves more with the spiritual sense of grace that comes as a gift from higher powers, whether as in the Voicework from the union of visceral and cerebral minds or from the inner connection of self with the infinite in yoga. This receptive state is reached in both disciplines through the agency of the breath. Kramer sheds light on the importance of breath in exploring asanas that again intersects with Fitzmaurice ideology: "The proper use of the breath gets you out of your mind and into your body, bringing grace and sensuality to movement impossible when the mind is in control" ("Self-Transformation" 4). Kramer's sensual approach shatters the denial concept that concerned Reich regarding yoga. It also seems to be a bridge in the reconciliation project called for by Lowen in traversing the body/spirit gap between bioenergetics and yoga.

SUBTLE BODY ANATOMY, TANTRA/DESIRE AND THE VOICEWORK

The Voicework, because it's a transformative system with therapeutic underpinnings and based in bioenergy, proposes to promote a fully integrated, holistically balanced actor. Part of that holism includes the subtle energy system known as prana, qi, ki or orgone. Following Asian metaphysical systems, these vital substances are contained in the air that one breathes. If this theory regarding energy transport is valid, then breath through inspiration leads to a connection between voice and the subtle body. The voice then is an expression of the subtle or etheric body as much as it is of the physical one, and thoughts or feelings traveling through both bodies flow through the voice. Through her personal encounters and experimentation with subtle energy, Fitzmaurice started to include such techniques as chakra awareness (see above, p. 61), aura reading and balancing in the Voicework. She states: "I started spontaneously to 'see' and sense stuff radiating and shooting around in my body and in others', and so I went to study meditation, Buddhism, healing and tantra, as I came across them – and one thing led naturally to another – I'd hear about this or that in discussion with people interested in similar phenomena – in order to make sense of my own experience" (E-mail to the author. 27 Sept. 2005). The premise underlying these methods is that the actor is enhanced in performance by having more access and flow from subtle body energy. From the physical to the super-physical, heightened reality parallels the operation of the voice in the heightened realm of the theater. According to Fitzmaurice:

> Heightened use of the voice and body in the theater requires making conscious choices for a particular result, for the audience to have a particular (and individual) experience – while maintaining economical and especially healthy functioning. This Voicework specifically gives tools for the actor to take care of himself while fulfilling the external demands (E-mail to the author. 29 Apr. 2006).

In order to draw a connection to the Voicework, it will be useful to gain a brief overview of the intricacy of energy anatomy. Initially, one must identify the astral or subtle body. Sylvan Muldoon offers a description in The Projection of the Astral Body:

> The Astral Body may be defined as the Double, or the ethereal counterpart of the physical body; which it resembles and with which it normally coincides. It is thought to be composed of some semi-fluidic or subtle form of matter, invisible to the physical eye…

> The broad, general teaching is that every human being 'has' an astral body just as he has a heart, a brain and a liver. In fact, the astral body is more truly the Real Man than the physical body is, for the latter is merely a machine adapted to functioning upon the physical plane (15).

Yoga's elaborate system of esoteric anatomy actually includes three major bodies or sheaths: the gross or physical, the astral or subtle, and the casual or seed body. These bodies are said to be vehicles for the soul or spirit. The casual body precedes and gives rise to the other two bodies. "This vehicle is comparatively permanent; its formation took place millions of years ago when the creature passed from the purely animal state to become a man. Since then it has been growing more or less, along with its physical body, which operates on the physical plane" (Swami Vishnudevananda

16). In yogic theory, the astral and physical bodies are linked. For this reason, one does not have to consciously activate the subtle body energy in order to influence it. Following this logic, activation of the gross and mental bodies, such as occur in bio-energetic destructuring or in yoga, would involve creating effects in the subtle body. Swami Vishnudevananda supports this when he states, "Though the physical body and the astral body are different, both are controlled by the mind" (259).

The subtle body, as noted above, is a "counterpart" to the physical body but is made of finer material and is invisible to normal sight. Its intimate correspondence with the physical body provides the theoretical basis for energy healing modalities as suggested by Richard Grossinger:

> The implications for healing are fundamental: if consciousness can root itself in a vehicle other that the physical body and can maintain continuity of ego-states, then the visible zone of the skeleton, viscera, sense organs, and flesh is merely one layer of our actual being – one layer for diseases to originate and lodge in and one layer in which to initiate cures. Diseases can also arise in the subtle body (as proposed by healers from Aboriginal Australia to ancient Greece) and can be treated and cured there. Much ethnomedicine and energy healing depends on some version of this cosmology (1: 317).

In yogic theory, subtle body anatomy includes a number of channels called *nadis* that course through the body on the astral plane and transport prana. The main channel called *sushumna nadi* starts from the base of the pelvis and moves along the center of the spine toward the top of the head. "More precisely the Central Conduit flows through the same space which on the physical level is taken up by the central sulcus of the spinal cord. Since these two structures exist on different levels of being they can occupy the same space simultaneously, an impulse in one often engendering an impulse in the other by resonance" (Lade and Svoboda 60). To the left and right respectively, *ida* and *pingala*– two other *nadis*–braid around *sushumna* to form a spiral-like caduceus-shaped staircase on their journey from the base of the spine to their destination at the mid-point between the two eyebrows.

Where the *ida* and *pingala nadis* intersect chakras are formed. The chakra *(see above p. 61)* is a center of concentrated subtle energy, and there are six of them along the path of the vertical spinal axis. The so-called seventh chakra, *sahasrara*, at the crown of the head, is not actually part of this arrangement since ida and pingala do not ascend that high. "Strictly speaking, it is not part of the *cakra* (Feurstein's spelling) system at all, but a body transcending locus where Consciousness appears to be connected to the human form" (Feuerstein 355). Sahasrara has this special designation as the entrance point for divine cosmic energy. Nevertheless, sahasrara is commonly listed with the chakras. Feuerstein defines the chakras as "pools of life energy, vibrating at different rates. Each cakra is associated with specific psychosomatic functions, but these energy whirls must not be confused with the nerve plexuses of the physical body with which they are, however, correlated" (353). The nadis transport prana; but in all except the advanced yogi, prana does not travel through the central *nadi*–the *sushumna*. The energy that resides at the base of the spine, at the bottom of the *sushumna nadi,* is called *kundalini.*

The pioneering British researcher of esoteric yoga, Sir John Woodroffe, a.k.a. Arthur Avalon offered this description in 1919 when he wrote, "Kundala means coiled. The power is the Goddess (Devi) Kundalini, or that which is coiled; for Her form is that of a coiled and sleeping serpent in the lowest body center, at the base of the spinal column, until by the means described She is aroused in that Yoga which is named after her. Kundalini is the Divine Cosmic Energy in bodies" (1). Iyengar locates the coiled serpent "two digits below the genital area and two above the anus" (Light on Pranayama 36). Kundalini is the manifestation of the goddess Shakti in the astral body. She represents creative energy or power and is the consort of Shiva–the masculine principle that represents pure consciousness. Kundalini epistemology is most prominent in the kind of yoga called tantra. The word literally means a loom or a weaving together. In tantric yoga, the adept seeks to raise Shakti up to the crown of the head where Shiva resides so the deified consorts can join. This symbolizes the weaving together of creative power with divine consciousness and is the goal of this yoga. When the prana is diverted from the ida and pingala channels through yogic practice to the sushumna, the serpent rises through each of the cakras as they open on its journey to the crown. Tantra, like other complex forms of yoga, utilizes asana, pranayama, mantra, meditation but is often distinguished by its emphasis on recovery of the feminine principle as *Devi- Shakti* (creative power), subtle body chakras, raising the kundalini, and sexual transmutation.

Tantra, a relatively recent development in the yogic psycho-spiritual technology emerging in India in the early part of the first millennium C.E., was the response to the question posed in The Yoga Tradition, "Why do we have to abandon pleasure in order to realize bliss?" (Feuerstein 341). It is important to distinguish two schools of tantric yoga–the right and the left. The more orthodox right school conforms to the traditional view of the yogi as an ascetic, spiritual devotee who relinquishes worldly activities in the pursuit of transcendence, while the left hand school promotes an approach that involves the student in the ways of the world in order to transcend them. One tantric scholar, David Frawley notes, "The right-handed path emphasizes meditational and spiritual disciplines and insists on a high degree of purity in conduct and action. The left-handed path employs various sexual practices or the use of meat and intoxicants which are not approved along the right-handed path" (38).

One could draw a connection with the Voicework and the left-handed school, because it's a practice that involves secular activity. Swami Ajaya supports that it is a way of life beyond the ashram:

> There is a branch of yoga called *Tantra*. Most people think that tantra yoga involves certain rituals, or has to do with the relationship between man and woman. But Tantra yoga can also be understood as an attitude toward all of life. In this practice instead of withdrawing from the world, going off and meditating, one uses the activities of the world as a means of centering the mind and expanding consciousness. Here we work with those things that ordinarily distract us. Instead of avoiding experiences with the attitude, 'here's something that ordinarily gets me involved, upset, or emotional, I'd better stay away from it.' Instead of running away from that experience that student chooses to become involved in it and learns to develop objectivity in the context of that situation. One may even seek out such a situation and practice centering the mind in the midst of it. From this perspective one should be able to maintain a meditative attitude in the midst of the most chaotic or potentially disturbing environment (Yoga Psychology 111-2).

There is, following this logic, a tantra of Fitzmaurice Voicework as an approach to unfolding and centering one's self in action. Tantra is nevertheless distinguished from the Voicework as an ecstatic technique of transcendence. "Tantra techniques bring sensuality into awareness so that it can become a means of transcending itself" (Rama, Ballentine, and Ajaya 236). Thus, engagement in worldly endeavors becomes a basis of detachment. As discussed previously, there is the inclusion of both detachment and commitment to expression in the Voicework that differentiates it from traditional yoga practice and this includes tantra.

Another connection to tantra yoga with Fitzmaurice Voicework is on the energetic level, intersecting with Reich's orgone theory. In a sense, tantra yoga parallels Reichian orgone therapy in casting sexuality in a prominent light as a means to holistic integration. In doing so, both systems alienated the traditional schools of thought that preceded them. Freud rejected Reich's orgastic potency theory, and that precipitated their estrangement. Similarly, the traditionalist schools of yoga condemned tantra as hedonistic. Both systems were considered to have a subversive element that potentially undermines the authority of societal morality by breaking the rules. Feuerstein notes "We still tend to think of sexuality and spirituality as incompatible, and hence we may be greatly offended by *gurus* who are sexually active" (344). This applies to psychotherapist type gurus as well as religious leaders. Significantly, however, both psychophysical approaches are plagued by misinterpretation. For example, neither Reichian therapy nor tantra yoga encourage promiscuity, and yet both of them were associated with the prior century's movement for sexual liberation in the West. Feuerstein attempts to clear up the confusion when he states, "The so-called sexual revolution of the 1960s and 1970s has, among other things, put Tantra on the map of our contemporary Western culture. Yet Tantra remains widely misunderstood and is often confused by Western neo-Tantrics with the Hindu erotic arts (kama-shastra)" (343). Such a distinction is equally applicable to Reichian therapy when it is miscast as a system promoting sexual licentiousness.

Reichian therapy and Voicework do not equate orgastic potency with ejaculation, and one could argue that there is a similar kind of transmutation of sexual energy into creative work, but the spiritual, internal aims dominate the tantric yogi to a degree that is not necessary for the actor. While there is expressive sublimation in the Voicework, there is certainly no restriction against physical orgasm in one's personal life, and this creates an important separation from tantra with its proscriptive approach toward sexuality. Although sexual congress is allowed in the left-hand school of tantra, there are clear and strict injunctions as well as ritual preparations. Importantly, no semen is lost. Instead, seminal fluid is transformed in a process of "inner alchemy" to a finer substance so it can be directed upward through the center of the spine to bring the participant to a state of enlightenment. Also, the female partner may not gain the same benefit, as she, in contrast, is permitted to reach orgasm but must supply that sexual essence for the male to absorb to further his kundalini's assent. This is clearly not Reich's orgasmic union since "The climax of Tantra yoga is not orgasm but ecstasy" (Feuerstein 366). While tantric yogis recognize, as did Reich, the primacy of sexual/creative energy, the destinations are distinct for the flow. In Reichian therapy, bioenergetics and Voicework, the energy is flowing throughout the body and out to the world. In tantra the energy is flowing up within the closed circuit of the subtle body. In the left-handed school, sexual energy is encountered not for gratification but for transmutation. The body is viewed as a mystical symbol, not a physical orgastic one. By making sex a metaphor, tantra takes it out of the physical body. The energy is the same but the construction is different. While there are levels and degrees of tantric practice, the basic direction of energy and focus is ultimately inward and upward. In the Voicework, there is a multi-directional focus and flow that, due to the specific need for communication, inevitably leads outward.

Because the Voicework includes tantric terminology, and in particular, the chakra system, it is important to understand this inclusion as a unique borrowing for vocal health and expression. The word chakra literally means wheel, and this connotation gives something of the active circulating qualities within them. It is important to clarify that yoga texts do not always agree in the details of what the actions and qualities are of the chakras. This is because, while they are considered real with standard locations in the subtle body, chakras are also paradigms for each yogi's spiritual evolution and are symbols for the stages of development that allow individual variation. The chakras are viewed as lotuses composed of petals. Swami Vishnudevananda gives the following identifications:

> There are six important *chakras*. They are: *muladhara*, containing four petals, located at the lower end of the spinal column; *swadhist-hana* (six petals), at the genital organs; *manipura* (ten petals) at the navel; *anahata* (twelve petals) at the heart; *vishudha* (sixteen petals) at the throat, and *ajna* (two petals) between the two eyebrows. The seventh chakra is known as *sahasrara*, which contains a thousand petals, located in the brain.
>
> In the physical body, the sacral plexus tentatively corresponds to *muladhara*; the prostatic plexus to *swadhisthana*; the solar plexus to *manipura*; the cardiac plexus to *anahata*; the laryngeal plexus to *vishudha*, and the cavernous plexus to *ajna* (296-7).

These are more commonly called in the west, consecutively, the root or anal, the genital, the solar plexus, the heart, the throat, the third eye and the crown chakras. Swami Vishnudevananda's tentative correlation is significant in that it cautions from equating the esoteric chakra system with the scientifically observable nervous system. In respecting the integrity of traditional yoga, there is no intercourse that doesn't risk adulteration from Western psychophysical approaches. The strict orthodoxy of any spiritual system retains a conservationist attitude in maintaining the sanctity of its structure.

David Frawley further qualifies these mergers as creating misconception:
> Much of New Age thought tends to identify the chakras with their physical counterparts. For example, if a person is highly emotional, it may be said that he or she has an open Heart Chakra. If a person has high sexual energy, he or she is said to have a strong Sex Chakra. Such statements relate to the physical functions which are reflections of the unopened astral chakras, not to the chakras in their opened condition. The chakras themselves only become active when the mind and Prana have entered into the Sushumna. This requires concentrated yogic practices and does not occur during ordinary consciousness.
>
> According to the yogic texts the chakras are closed in all people except those who have practiced deep meditation...The chakras are misinterpreted when we look at them primarily on the physical level. For example, sexual activity is a function of the physical organs. It is not the function of the awakened Earth or Water Chakras, which give detachment from the organs of reproduction and elimination. Increasing the activity of the physical organs does not aid in developing the chakras but depresses their function, as their energy is directed outwardly and into physical matter, not into the inner consciousness (179).

If one takes Frawley's sobering argument into consideration, the inclusion of chakras into other systems of psychophysical development must occur mostly on a metaphoric level, where they can operate as centers of awareness for growth. In Fitzmaurice Voicework, chakra balancing is done as a diagnostic method to assess the energetic flow within the student. In addition, the Voicework includes vocalizing while visualizing the chakras in the transition from destructuring to restructuring. As such it is an ordering system towards expression. While this differs from the traditional opening of the chakras in the meditative mode as described by Frawley, he gives a metaphysical basis for sound production that provides fertile imagery for the actor's voice when he writes, "According to Tantra the mind consists primarily of sound. Working with sound, whether as mantra, music or vibration is central to energization of the mind" (55).

In the tantra tradition, there are four levels of speech, which correspond to the throat, heart, navel and root centers. In yoga, speech and sound have a highly spiritual dynamic and typically is at odds with the worldly communication of the Western theater. But in the Voicework, a potential bridge occurs since the spirit of sound, which is not limited to yogic practice, is reified in destructuring sessions that employ a rich imagery of an inner world. Fitzmaurice may not stress the spiritual aspect, but the symbolism resonates with the Voicework in a passage from Frawley in the following consideration, "The power of speech must be brought down to the base of the spine (root chakra) to allow the energy of consciousness to ascend upward as Kundalini to awaken our higher potentials. Before our consciousness ascends, our energy must first descend and penetrate to the depths of our being" (55). Such inducements interface neatly with the Voicework's purpose of creating an integrated, multi-leveled expressive actor. In this way, tantra yoga provides a context from which the Voicework borrows in order to assist the actor to discover varied psycho-emotional centers for sound.

The discussion of chakras will, therefore, focus on those applications most pertinent to the Voicework. A particularly potent description, applicable to the theater, can be found in Psychotherapy East and West:

> These centers are called *chakras*. The English words 'circle' and 'circus' are derived from the Sanskrit word 'chakra.' A circus is a circular arena with tiers and seats in which public entertainment takes place. Similarly, each chakra is an area in which a particular form of entertainment or drama occurs. Typically, one is involved in the drama, but if one develops his powers of self-observation, it is possible to become a spectator of the grand show that occurs at each chakra. The word 'circus' also refers to a circular area where many streets intersect. In the same way, each chakra is a center at

which many forces intersect in a human being. Each chakra may be likened to the hub of a wheel, with spokes radiating outward from the center. The forces that radiated out from each chakra affect one's physical, emotional, and psychical functioning (Ajaya 243).

This theatrical rendering provides stimulation for the discussion. In the Voicework, as in meditation, the seeker/player is always given the choice about entering or detaching from the arenas of life. In the Voicework, one seeks a balance between observation and action, and the chakra imagery yield rich fields for inner play, transformation and growth. The symbolism contained within the chakras is too dense for a study of this kind. Therefore, the discussion will be limited to a few of the junctures that apply to the Voicework from a theoretical standpoint. One of the strengths of this work is to give space to actors to find their own voice and develop the path to their own techniques within a context that provides guideposts but not rigid impositions. Such over-structuring would suggest a current of ideology that moves counter to the very core of a system designed to challenge rigidities in favor of fluidity. The experimental spirit of the work allows admission for diversity and individual response within a defined progression. While Fitzmaurice views the chakras as an ordering system, the actual construction of that order is founded upon a unique personal resonance to each center of awareness, since the building materials emerge from the individual psyche and body with the guidance of the teacher.

Significantly, Reich located seven areas of armoring that provide an ordering system for viewing and destructuring the body. While these correspond somewhat to the cakra system, they do not form a complete equation with that system. Yet for the Fitzmaurice teacher, awareness of both systems allows for a textured perspective of the body that affords more layered opportunities for shifting energy and opening space for sound. Reich noted, "In carefully examining typical cases of various illness in the search for a law that governs these blocks, I discovered that the muscular armor is arranged in segments" (Character 369). One can draw some interesting hypothetical links between the segments and chakras. Particularly, there are possible alignments between the first segment-the ocular with the 6th /the third eye chakra, the second segment-the oral armor ring and the third segment-the pharynx with the 5th/the throat chakra, the fourth segment-the chest with the 4th/heart chakra, and the fifth segment-the diaphragm with the 3rd /the solar plexus chakra. The sixth segment, including the rectus abdominus, transverses abdominus, latissimus dorsi and sacrospinalis, is a large area that does not fit the one pointed centrality of the chakra system. Reich's seventh segment is the pelvis that contains both the second and first chakras.

The first chakra is significant to the Voicework, because it connects with the instinct for survival that figures in with the primal fight/flight responses of the organism. The induced tremor in Fitzmaurice Voicework, by its very nature, harmonizes with this chakra, which is associated with fear and particularly fear of death. The tremoring experience, in essence, dismantles the structuring forces inhibiting life flow and unleashes the emotional issues surrounding them. According to Voicework theory, by grounding the voice in the root chakra, one is permitting the instinctive content that resides there to well up. Through tremoring, one is also unleashing the animalistic resources of survival. Both vulnerability and power, through tremoring while visualizing the root chakra, infuse the voice, and the vibrations of sound synergistically unlock the energies inherent to this center. Flow and focus interplay in an energetic dialogue as consciousness is summoned into this chakra, where insight is transformed through the inner shifts of the tremor that become the building materials for navigating the fear of change and its most profound manifestation–the fear of death. It is here in the field of the first cakra that one learns about the holding mechanisms designed to ward off the fear of death. This parallels the fear of change that figures in the actor's navigation through transitions and by the anxiety known as stage fright. By bringing awareness into the physical location of the root chakra while experiencing the palpable agitation of the tremor, one comes to understand the psychophysical dynamics that attempt to prevent change as well as the survival mechanism of adaptation and surrender that permit change to become an ally rather than an enemy. This occurs when the struggle shifts from resistance to flow.

It is the permission to open up to all experience that also ultimately empowers the actor's voice as one transitions from destructuring to restructuring. Transitions, or Keleman's "middle ground" (77) become opportunities for the actor to let go in order to continue or survive. The "little death" or orgasm is metaphoric for the surrender into flow and is re-echoed in Krishnamurti's support for the positive essential spirit of change, whether manifesting as life or death, through his inducement to embrace "endless movement" (77). For the tremoring actor, therefore, the lesson of the first chakra involves an understanding of the spirit of survival through embracing transitions.

There is an autonomic reaction to fear that involves the opening of the sphincter muscles that underscores the primal nature of this chakra, noted in Yoga and Psychotherapy. "It is interesting that anatomically, this center is in the area of the anus and is associated with the excretion of solid matter from the body. When animals are observed in frightening situations, it will be seen that defecation is one of the main components of their fear response" (Rama, Ballentine, and Ajaya 228-9). The correlation of this chakra to the anus links to Freudian and Reichian therapies where that site is implicated in early traumas around toilet training that manifest later in an array of neurotic characteristics. Such traumas may be textured into the psychophysical patterning within this area of the body that is reflected in the inability to eliminate and let go on the emotional level. For the actor, old unconscious memories of fear around 'letting go' buried at this site can intensify the experience of stage fright to the point where creativity is seriously compromised. In the Voicework by going into this center that "lays the foundations for psychic organization" (Rama, Ballentine, and Ajaya 229), one is learning to release and make choices about harnessing this energy in productive ways. The fertility of the process is emphasized in the transformative agenda of yoga that applies to the Voicework as stated in Yoga and Psychotherapy, "Psychological growth is based on the process of continually bringing into awareness parts of oneself that were before regarded as repulsive and unsavory, so that they can become integrated and transmuted" (230). There is more active engagement and participation through emotional responsiveness in the destructuring phase of the Voicework, but the blueprint for transmutation is the same. The aims, of course, can vary, since the yogi may choose to restructure towards inner peace and seclusion while the actor must always choose a restructuring path that brings one into outward relationships.

The issue of relationships brings one to the second chakra, which contain the drama of sexuality, biological creativity and play. Because of the intrinsic potency associated with this chakra and societal prohibitions imposed upon the sexual impulses that this chakra represents, the drama here can be quite intense. It is the chakra that is affiliated with Freud and Reich, since sexuality undergirds their therapies. Swami Ajaya notes:

> Wilhelm Reich and Alexander Lowen also view human existence from the perspective of the second chakra. Their psychologies emphasize the capacity to experience sensory pleasure as the measure of a human being's fulfillment. They emphasize the positive

aspects of this mode of experience and assert that a human being should fully experience his capacity for orgasm. Their therapies focus on removing muscular and characterological blocks and inhibitions in order to increase one's experience of pleasure. The methods they use can help one achieve that end, but their therapies neglect to look beyond the pleasure principle to recognize the significance of other realms of experience (Psychotherapy 258).

While this is a somewhat reductive view of these therapies, Ajaya goes on to credit them with understanding the significance of pleasure beyond the pursuit of objects of desire:

> But if one learns to relax and experience his own organism rather than pursuing something outside himself, he will find that the experience of pleasure is inherent in that relaxed state. Then he will experience that intense sensory pleasure that is already a part of one's being and is not dependent upon uniting with an external object. Reich was aware of this. In his therapy, he emphasized the relaxation of chronically tense muscles and the capacity to experience intense sensory pleasure throughout one's body, independent of external objects (Psychotherapy 259).

The Voicework, being inclusive, garners this insight from exploration of the second chakra, but it also creates a constructive field of play for the actor to allow sensuality as well as sexuality to infuse the voice in relationship with others. The modus operandi is the same as the exploration for all the chakras, that is, visualizing and destructuring, but the tremor positions change to correspond with each chakra. This is because of precise physical emphases that the positions highlight.

The third chakra, located at the navel, corresponds to skill, mastery, technique, discipline and ego. In the Voicework, because of its location, it is significant for the connection with the transverses muscle, diagrammatic center, solar plexus and the breath. In yogic theory it resonates with fire, oxidation and "the power to destroy and create (the world)…" (Avalon 369). Because this chakra contains the energy of competition, the focus on its imagery may create the stimulus for empowering one to pursue the actions that lead to winning. But it is important to keep in mind that the Voicework, through the tremor positions and the focus of mental and breath energy into any of the chakra areas, leaves an open field of discovery for the actor. While there are traditional significations to each chakra that often resonate in a very harmonizing way with the Voicework, the intention is generally not to impose the ancient symbolism on the individual but to give the permission to tap into and to discover a personal history that may also reverberate on a more universal level. In the Voicework, this is the breathing chakra and because of this basic life giving quality, the empowering center.

The fourth chakra is regarded as the point of transition between biological needs and higher consciousness (Rama, Ballentine, and Ajaya 243). The heart chakra relates to compassion for others and a shift from self-involvement. It is a center for synthesis and integration of lower and higher centers and therefore represents a point of transformation and embodies the essence of yogic synthesis. As the chakra preceding it, the heart chakra has a special connection with the breath because of its location immediately above it. Whereas the third chakra utilizes oxygen to empower, the fourth uses breath in the inner alchemy of transformation. "This sort of feeling and emotion marks a departure from the biological and survival concerns which are related to the lower three chakras. The diaphragm serves as a boundary between the lower, and more instinctual nature of man, and the higher centers which become increasingly related to a more evolved consciousness" (Rama, Ballentine, and Ajaya 244). In the Voicework, the fourth chakra takes on the special importance of being the center of heart-felt communication.

The fifth or throat chakra, beyond the obvious connection to the Voicework as a source of communication, is also a center of nourishment and receptivity. The notion of receptivity figures well with the Voicework's undertaking of opening and relaxing the throat. This task is utilized to offset the habits of pushing and tensing. The message is that creativity is bred from receptivity; that the air coming in, and with it, the ideas that lead to inspiration must nourish the actor. Nourishment relates to the oral stage in Reichian therapy and this chakra's location may hold memories of such oral expressions as sucking, biting, and spitting. Through nourishment, the fifth chakra maintains an affinity to personal growth. The authors of Yoga and Psychotherapy distinguish yoga from the psychoanalytical model by emphasizing a "growth-oriented" rather than a "illness-oriented" focus:

> The paranoid state involves fear of the ego being lost or swallowed
> up in a regression to a more primitive undifferentiated stage of
> development; while in yoga, the longing and seeking associated with

the throat chakra relates to the ego searching for some 'nurturance from above,' for some contact with a higher potential, some way to outgrow itself. The former is associated with the intense oral craving which leads to both the desire to engulf and the fear of engulfment. The latter is the search for guidance from a consciousness beyond one's present limits (257).

There is an essential bonding between yoga and Voicework in this growth orientation that reifies in the fifth chakra. Bioenergetics may also have this potential, but Lowen, as a doctor, was primarily concerned with treating disease in patients. Penelope Court argues that acting training needs to be more open in acknowledging its therapy base and that it should be embraced rather than qualified, suggesting that the neurotic actor is less capable of meeting the demands of a rigorous development program (12-3). This is difficult to confirm since acting training does not fall under the rubric of exact measurable science. It is an old debate that questions if the actor cured of neurosis would also lose the spurs that ignite and sometimes equate with talent. In response, Fitzmaurice focuses on setting high standards for growth that reflexively may hold healing benefits. She does not explicitly speak to the actors about their own life beyond the voice class, nor does she shy away from it. But importantly, she does not design her work around the cure of neurosis as much as she does around healthy growth potential.

Yoga, too, is not actually focused on healing disease, although this may be a benefit of self-evolution on a path that is growth oriented. Joel Kramer notes, "Growth almost always involves a shattering of self-images, a major shift in one's habitual life patterns" ("Mind in Asana" 21). But in most Western psychotherapy, the start point is problematic; there is a complex, a dysfunction, and an inability to cope. Often the purpose of such therapy is to help the person adjust to what are considered acceptable norms of society. While Freudian psychoanalysis may accentuate this negative starting point, there is frequently the same implication of abnormality in much psychotherapy, including bioenergetics as the authors of Yoga and Psychotherapy note, "Psychoanalysis emphasizes repression because its interest is in how mental illness originates. Yoga psychology, however, is more interested in providing a way of understanding even the well-adapted mind so that development will not be limited to what is currently considered 'normal'" (110). Fitzmaurice is not particularly interested in bringing the actor's voice to what might be considered normal, although health and naturalness is of prime importance. However, due to the special demands of the acting arena, the Voicework aims to explore the extraordinary in vocal expression. Similarly, the demands of yoga therapy constitute a calling for the extraordinary that resonates with the actor who wishes to grow beyond a comfortable normalcy:

> The throat chakra is the focus of vocalization and singing, of verbalization and creativity. Traditionally in yoga, artists and musicians are said to have their energy concentrated here. It is through sound vibrations, word and verbal symbols that we create our world ... Through the repetition of verbal ritual, one's reality can be restructured and recreated. New words and new thoughts create a new world, at least temporarily (Rama, Ballentine, and Ajaya 259).

The call to restructuring and creativity moving one beyond the known is an important aspect of the Voicework.

Yet, there is a distinction in the fact that yoga may privilege the higher centers to the demotion of the ego driven lower chakras, whereas the Voicework looks to embody and empower all centers as fitting the flexibility of the actor's psyche and voice for character transformation. The Voicework is an approach that theoretically interfaces with this evocation of higher vocal realities, growing from the exposure to deep inner journeys reaching to new insights that prompt expression. In this way, the Voicework relates to the fifth chakra in the evocation of the "inner voice" (Rama, Ballentine and Ajaya 261):

> In the act of being creative, one nurtures himself by giving himself and accepting for himself the guidance from the higher consciousness that lies within...When consciousness is first focused at the throat chakra, one's role is still that of the receiver of 'grace.' The ability to receive grace is a step above the capacities of the heart chakra where one is limited to being compassionate, to sharing as a separate being with a limited other. Now, instead, one is able to accept from an inner, unlimited source (262).

The fifth chakra, as the symbol of nourishment, becomes not only the expressive center but also the womb for new possibilities beyond the limitations of habit-run speech. In this natural progression of growth, it becomes the matrix for the higher consciousness embodied in the sixth and seventh chakras.

The inner voice of the fifth chakra is paralleled by the inner vision of the sixth. The third eye has a traditional designation as the seat of intuition. In Yoga and Psychotherapy it is noted that, "Consciousness that is centered at the *ajna* chakra involves 'introspection' or 'the ability to see within.'...This is a deeper vision or intuitive means of gaining knowledge" (264). In Fitzmaurice Voicework this chakra corresponds to an imagined outlet for communicative energy streaming forward to an external focus point. It is a cultivating center where inner focus communes with outer focus. The transforming focus-line is a place of refinement where the flow of information from the lower chakras is clarified through insight on its journey out toward the world. Sensations and emotions receive illumination on this line in order to clarify the communication of sound and speech. Yoga makes a distinction between *buddhi*–higher mind–and *manas*–lower mind. Buddhi is equivalent to reason and wisdom. The concept of buddhi corresponds to the development of choice in the restructured actor. It involves creating and re-creating modes of communication, and, in Fitzmaurice Voicework, the challenge is to always interrogate reason via destructuring. In yoga, the journey is toward a separation between these two minds as the consciousness evolves toward detachment from the realm of sensory input that characterizes the lower mind. This yogic journey leads one to a "vantage point" (Rama, Ballentine, and Ajaya 98) where the mind can observe and distance itself from the lower churnings of agitated thoughts. By contrast, the Voicework may initially separate, then merge and play the edges of the two minds, causing a dynamic intuitive center that is fluid and pointed alternately in a way that is analogous to quantum theory's particle and wave.

The seventh chakra, the center of cosmic consciousness, having obvious divine connotations, most links to the Voicework through the notion of union in vocal expressiveness through performance, where the actors are flowing in harmony of play with each other and the audience. It stands for the accomplishment of a holistic, deeply centered and charged vocal communication that is informed both by inner and outer wisdom. Saul Kotzubei, a Fitzmaurice Voicework master teacher makes the following comment on its relevance to his work:

> My thoughts about union and the voice here, is that we can also
> be talking about a union between the actor, their expressivity (as
> voice), the other actors, the space, the story, the audience (or I sup-
> pose the camera and mike), in short the whole of the phenomenal

plane as represented by the space in theatre (or studio) so that through the expression of the 7th chakra, one is in some sense (re) creating the experience of the divine as the union of all things, the cosmic union as expressed by the interpenetration of phenomena, more specifically the massive interpenetration of vibrations, in which all are engulfed, in which all are affected" (E-mail to the author. 30 Oct. 2005).

One route where the seventh chakra intersects with the Voicework is through the healing system outlined by Barbara Ann Brennan. Brennan was a NASA physicist who later directed her interests to psychotherapy and healing. She instructed Fitzmaurice in the study of human energy systems. Brennan's healing work is based in a synthesis of the yogic subtle energy anatomy with bioenergetics and core energetic therapy. The theoretical underpinning for her work is further advanced by the holographic model as described by the physicist, David Bohm, in his book The Implicate Order (183). Holographic unity, where the whole is contained in the part, provides the foundation for Brennan's treatment of the physical body through the etheric or subtle body double, since these linked parts contain the whole human being (Brennan 25). Yet it is important to credit Fitzmaurice with the specific connection of the chakra system and voice for the actor:

> Reich himself was somewhat, but not significantly, aware of oriental philosophies and therapies, but had no interest in theatre or theatre training. Neither bioenergetics nor core energetics nor Barbara Brennan's healing science school, which I attended for 6 years, are connected with theatre in any way. So I do believe that bringing these concepts to voice training was entirely my idea, though there are some other significant contributions with a similar scope now. I taught workshops at the ATHE conference from 78 to 98, which launched these ideas widely in the United States. In 98 I offered a workshop at ATHE on voice and healing, and the idea was taken up for the whole VASTA conference. My Barbara Brennan school undergraduate (99) and graduate (01) theses were on this connection: a discussion of the holistic voice, in theatre and in life – 5th chakra healing (E-mail to author. 29 Apr. 2006).

Brennan provides a model for destructuring and restructuring on the etheric level. In this model, the healer/teacher is a medium for the transmission of subtle energies from higher consciousness both into and out of the patient/student's body. She contributes techniques of chakra and aura diagnosis and cleansing. The eye and hand of the healer are prominent in the use of these modalities for analysis and treatment. In her system, the eye is trained to see auras. Fitzmaurice employs this in her own practice, but it is not typically part of her teacher training. Fitzmaurice understands that the complexity of Brennan's system requires specific techniques to develop the abilities of seeing and sensing energy fields. While this method is an extremely valuable asset for the Fitzmaurice trained teacher, it constitutes a special category of study within the Voicework's technology. It is more of an advanced skill that could be useful in further reading the body, clearing or destructuring it of blockage, and restructuring it in a more energetically flowing dynamic configuration. To be a truly masterful teacher in the Fitzmaurice tradition, in addition to having an in-depth understanding of the special needs of the actor's voice, one would also have an in-depth practical understanding of bioenergetics, yoga, subtle energetic bodywork and shiatsu.

FITZMAURICE VOICEWORK AND SHIATSU

Shiatsu is a Japanese method of finger or thumb pressure applied to specific points on the body. The treatment, however, can be extended to include other means of application including the hands, forearms, elbows, knees and feet. In addition to point pressure, the shiatsu practitioner may use a variety of techniques involving kneading, rolling, shaking, pulling, rocking, and stretching the body of the receiver. The official definition given by the Japanese Ministry of Health is "a manipulation ... without the use of any instrument, mechanical or otherwise, to apply pressure to the human skin, correct internal malfunctioning, promote and maintain health and treat specific diseases" (Drury 190). Therefore, Shiatsu is a healing modality on a par with ancient systems predating the development of modern medicine's reliance on drugs and surgery.

Shiatsu is based in the Chinese system of finger pressure called *Tao-Yinn*, which translates as *Do-In* in Japanese. Do-In, a method of self-massage, is usually distinguished from shiatsu, which can be either self-applied or administered to a receiving person. It is related to acupuncture, but shiatsu utilizes no needle insertion. Shiatsu shares with traditional Chinese medicine a view that the body is mapped with an energetic grid called the meridian system. There are twelve main meridians named after the internal organs that they correspond to such as heart, lung, kidney, large intestine, etc. These meridians run vertically along the arms and legs bilaterally. There are also eight "extraordinary" meridians, of which the two main ones, the Governor and Conception vessels, run vertically up along the midline of the back and down the midline of the anterior aspect of the body respectively. These meridians arise to the surface of the body but have deep connections to the organ systems with which they are affiliated. It is because of this affiliation that the meridians are utilized for therapeutic effect to contact and alter the interior condition of the body. Traditional Chinese medical theory holds that the meridians are conveyers of *qi* (pronounced 'chee'), a term that is often translated as vital energy or life force. The places where the *qi* collects at precise locations on the surface of the skin along the meridians are called acupoints. There are 361 meridian points and 40 extra points that are listed in the authoritative text, <u>Chinese Acupuncture and Moxibustion</u> (108). The extra points have very specific health indications and may or may not be located on the channels. Many of these channel and non-channel points are utilized in shiatsu. Shiatsu has foundations in Chinese meridian theory; however, the practice is not solely limited to acupoints or extra points but may be expanded to include any tender spots that are called *Ashi* points in traditional Chinese medicine.

In Shiatsu, all the points of contact are simply called *tsubo* and the vital energy that they contain is called *ki* (pronounced 'key'), which for all intents and purposes is interchangeable with the Chinese term *qi*. Saul Goodman, a master shiatsu practitioner and the author of <u>The Book of Shiatsu</u>, defines tsubo as "Where the cycling of electromagnetic energy gathers. A tsubo might be compared to a volcano, where energy deep within the earth's core rises to the surface and is released. Likewise, tsubos are places where energy is particularly active and interchanging with the environment" (1-3). Accordingly, Fitzmaurice Voicework employs therapeutic touch in addition to tremoring as another means of releasing the free flow of creative energy and channels it into the voice as it interchanges with the environment. Touch is used in these systems to contact the core of the person. In bioenergetics, the core is seen as the essential self below the layers of the protective personality and subterranean neurotic drives. It is the deep essence of vitality that connects Pierrakos' core of positive self-expression with the yogi's infinite inner Self. Touch, in Voicework and in shiatsu is a way of communicating with the interior. Prior to Fitzmaurice, although Reich and

Lowen did not call it shiatsu, they had already moved in the direction of therapeutic touch by dissolving chronic rigidities in the body of their patients:

> Prior to leaving for Switzerland, an important development occurred in Reichian therapy – the use of direct contact with the patient's body to release muscular tensions which blocked his ability to give in to his feelings and allow the orgasm reflex to take place. During his work with me Reich occasionally applied pressure with his hands to some of the tense muscles in my body to help them relax. Usually, with me and with others, he applied such pressure to the jaw...As a result, the breathing becomes freer and deeper, and often involuntary tremors occur in the body and legs (Lowen Bioenergetics 26).

Fitzmaurice Voicework intersects with shiatsu at several ideological junctions. Like many Asian healing modalities, shiatsu seeks for energetic balance and, in this way, corresponds to the process of synthesis that occurs when the actor integrates connections from destructuring with the restructuring phases in the Voicework. In both systems, balance constitutes a recovery and return to nature:

> Now twentieth-century man is discovering what was common understanding in the ancient world. One wonders why our modern schools refer to our ancestors as primitive and uncivilized. In its real sense 'primitive' means those that understand the balance and harmony of nature and base their thought, expression and way of life upon it. Real shiatsu is like this. It is an expression of making balance, the basic activity of nature. It is approaching life with deep respect and acknowledging that all humans and animals, as well as the vegetable world, elemental world and energy spheres, are related and interdependent. It is acknowledging that making balance is common and essential to life (Goodman 7).

Both shiatsu and the Voicework bring about balance through engaging the autonomic nervous system so that the person emerges with new choices about behavior. Additionally, the therapeutic concepts surrounding touch in shiatsu can be equally applied to the Voicework. In both systems, touch is used diagnostically to determine energy patterns and as such constitute a form of body reading with the goal of developing fine-tuned sensitization to what Saul Goodman calls "invisible systems". He explains that:

> When shiatsu is given, stimulation at the skin surface triggers a response of the nervous system. This effects a reaction and change in the meridians and chakras. Together these changes create adjustments of the body chemistry, systems and organs. The changing, adjusting meridian and chakra energy conversely influences the nervous system which in turn alters the skin response to the stimulus (22- 3).

Goodman's model of the autonomic nervous system, dividing into the orthosympathetic and parasympathetic, has *ortho* corresponding to left brain functions and *para* to right brain functions (25). Therefore, this division distinguishes the ortho system involved with analytical brain activity from the para system that has more to do with the right brain function of synthesis. From this particular perspective, the ortho has a strong affinity with consciousness, while the para represents the entire subconscious internal activities of the autonomic nervous system. It is debatable, however, that consciousness is limited to the ortho, or conversely, that some of the functions that occur there are not unconscious. Nor is one always unaware of parasympathetic responses. This is a functional representation of the nervous system, and not a rigorously scientific one. Goodman is setting up a working model where he equates the orthosympathetic system with the sensory and motor branch of the peripheral nervous system that innervates the skin. This includes the sympathetic network of nerve cells that regulate sweat glands, blood vessels and hair follicles as well as the other sensory mechanisms in the skin that detect pressure, pain, pleasure and temperature. Because he includes the tension of fight/flight responses under the orthosympathetic system heading, the parasympathetic system, by contrast, correlates with relaxation. Following Goodman's model, the sympathetic nervous system (ortho) dominates the surface of the body, and the parasympathetic governs the deep interior of the body:

> The orthosympathetic system or mode is connected more to the surface of the body and its activity relates to separation and discrimination of distinct sensory perceptions, along with responses to tension. When the branch is more active, body and meridian energies are more distinguished and specified in function. Ortho

also tends to influence expenditure and dissipation of energy. The parasympathetic system or mode is more involved with the deep body processes, and its activation provides a unifying experience of body, mind, spirit and environment. When para is more active, energies tend to merge, balance, regenerate and function as a whole (25).

When pressure is applied through shiatsu, the ortho system is initially alerted and goes into action by identifying and isolating the precise sensations belonging to the touch. This discriminating function of the orthosympathetic arouses the fight/flight mechanism of the body as the quality of the pressure is analyzed to determine the nature of the response. "The receiver is consciously aware of a single point: resistance" (Goodman 25). The reaction to touch is significant in determining the next level of experience and depends both on the sensitization of the giver and the particular character of the receiver's body/mind complex:

Once this system, which is related to the body's defense mechanism or 'fight or flight' response, is satisfied that the stimulus is not potentially harmful to the survival of the organism, its activity diminishes and recedes. The effect of the stimulus will then be transmitted by the para mode which allows it to be experienced beyond the point of contact and eventually by the whole body. Therefore when the activation of ortho recedes, the sensation at the point of contact is integrated into the body's entire system and experienced via the para system" (Goodman 26).

In traditional Chinese medical theory, the protective qi called *wei qi* runs along the outside of the body in the layers of the skin. It is the body's first defense against invasive pathogenic factors and is important in retaining the integrity of the body's immune system. Goodman explores the fight/flight dynamic from the perspective of touch, and it is congruent with this traditional Chinese medical (TCM) theory. Significantly, the *wei qi* is controlled by the lung that governs respiration, and it is almost universal practice in therapeutic body techniques and in the Voicework to encourage the receiver to breathe as a way of meeting stress. This symbolically extends to encountering rehearsal and performance stress and becomes an important reflex for the actor under pressure. In Fitzmaurice Voicework, the breath serves as a messenger of integration between the two systems governing the surface of the skin and the interior of the body as described by Goodman. It is important to understand that in the Voicework, touch, which can arouse the fight/flight mechanism with induced stress reactions, can also provide the antidote of reassurance, relaxation and calm. In the Voicework, this depends on the same characteristics involved in shiatsu such as degree and duration of pressure, location and the mental/emotional state of the receiver and giver. While there is a degree of passivity in the reciprocity of touch, the receiver is active in terms of the breath, and it is here that the actor most benefits from such contact, since the integration gained through tactile stimulation is toward dynamic utilization in vocal expression and performance. In his explanation, the progressive touch moves from the surface to the interior, from isolation to integration. Goodman's thesis suggests that the consciousness of the surface recedes as the interior comes into play and opens the realm of the unconscious; the place where deep learning and shifting of patterns can take place. Because in Fitzmaurice Voicework the student may be tremoring concurrently with shiatsu touch instead of the sympathetic system receding "into the background", a more complex situation can be engendered where tremoring underground and touch on the surface create an alternation of para/sympathetic foregrounding and backgrounding within the matrix of experience. This can lead to an overall relaxation if the para system prevails, causing energy flow as Goodman describes or more active involvement of impulses, which can also flow spontaneously if the sympathetic is foregrounded. Ideally, the student is able to flow between one system and the other without resistance in a flood of creative activity and reactivity.

In Goodman's technique, after initial contact, the practitioner is encouraged to "sink more deeply to the bottom of the point", which he clarifies may only be a "fraction of an inch" (28). This process fits with the Voicework in plumbing the actor's psyche via the body. Goodman gives the following two reasons why this sinking technique is beneficial: "First, the whole body is then receiving the stimulus. Second, by connecting this point with the whole body energy system, the point is then nourished and revitalized by an influx of energy" (29). This whole body energy occurs on a vibrational level and is further enhanced by the use of sound vibrations. The Voicework builds on this theory to charge the whole body toward dynamic flow that is both supportive of and nourished by sound production.

Goodman uses the lock of a canal to analogize the opening of the body–the freeing from tension and the switch from sympathetic to parasympathetic:

> We can get a feeling for how the body energy works in accord
> with the autonomic nervous system by comparing it to the lock
> system of a canal. When we feel relaxed due to a more dominant
> para mode, energy begins to flow freely, encouraging excesses
> of energy in one area or meridian to dissipate while deficient
> places regenerate. The body and all its deep life processes are
> balanced and revitalized. This is similar to when the locks of
> a canal open, letting water flow between the sections, thus bal-
> ancing the water levels and allowing the movement of a vessel
> between the locks (26-7).

His analogy corresponds to focus and attention when locked and not flowing in a Voicework session, and must be distinguished from relaxed alertness and the kind of focus point that permits energetic fluidity. In the Voicework, both tremoring and touch are used as paths to the interior where creative flow is the desired outcome. In Goodman's model, fight/flight mechanisms are antithetical to the full body relaxation responses of the parasympathetic autonomic system, but in the Voicework fight/flight reactions retain importance in conjunction with the surrender involved in relaxing. Since the actor's voice must be open to both kinds of expression, the balance evolved must include a focus that is alert and connected to survival instincts with the deep body wisdom of relaxation that moves toward complex integration and coordination that is both mental and physical. Ideally, this balance plays out in such a way that alertness does not create an excess of paralyzing tension, and relaxation does not create a mental deficiency that results in the total lethargy and unconsciousness of sleep. The theory of excess and deficiency are cornerstones to traditional Chinese medicine and are borrowed by Goodman to explain shiatsu's underlying goal for balance:

> Once the whole body relaxes and energy is freely moving through
> the various systems, more specific balances and alignments
> are made available to us through working with specific points,
> meridians, muscles and manipulations. It is like opening the
> door to a house. Once we enter we can move freely about the
> rooms, rearranging them or changing their appearance if we

wish. In shiatsu, getting the receiver to relax, open, and trust our touch is the initial step in treatment. Assisting the reorganization of energy is the second step and can only be done if the first is accomplished (29).

There is an energetic fluidity within that reflects in the outer world as shiatsu prepares the receiver for contacts with life beyond the therapeutic session. The body in relationship to its environment parallels the stage of restructuring. To spin off of Goodman's thesis in terms of Fitzmaurice Voicework, if inner chaos leads to order and a micro/macrocosmic connection is valid, then inner and outer aspects of the body continuously interfaces with larger cosmic order. The actor then becomes a sensitized barometer to these shifts and changes that open up the wealth of experiences such interconnections offer:

> When we study the body and its relationship to the environment, we discover that its form and function, including the meridian system, are products of environmental order. In a sense we are directly plugged into nature via our energy system. This means that the energy system, nervous system, blood and hormone system etc., react to and interchange with weather patterns, ion changes, planetary and constellation movements. When the environment changes on any level from social circumstances to natural phenomena, such as a drop in the barometric pressure, our complete energy field adapts to make balance. Physically, emotionally, and psychologically we are immediately influenced. Even our judgment, actions and decisions can be altered (Goodman 31).

While this theory operates as a metaphoric spur to the actor's receptivity and expressiveness, there is also some scientific basis through the fundamental law of cause and effect. In this vision of wholeness, there is a harmonic bridge to Reich's cosmic orgone theory and the agreement nourishes the substratum of the Voicework that anchors it as a system with multi-leveled potentials. The voice, following this theory, literally extends itself to energetic realms beyond the gross dimensions of physical reality. The interchangeability of matter and energy growing out of modern physics supports the ancient mystical traditions and finds a territory that is mutually fertilized from both

East and West in the exploration through the Voicework that keeps an open mind and body to each.

In this vocal experience, communication may equate with communion. Goodman offers a definition that applies to the Voicework, "Commune or communion means 'becoming one'. In giving shiatsu, we develop our sense of oneness" (38). He is referring to the nature of the relationship that is cultivated in the exchange of energy between giver and receiver. This relationship in shiatsu also provides a paradigm that is applicable to that of two actors in a scene or the actor/audience bond. These correlations may be further textured through the inclusion of sound in the Voicework. A restructuring of energy is possible in this exchange based on the degree of release and the permission to physically and emotionally allow one to touch and be touched by another. The lessons learned in the deep mode of the autonomic system's understanding of stress and relaxation become guideposts that inform the quality of exchange between giver and receiver whether they are teacher and student, or health practitioner and client, or actor and audience. A model of behavior is learned in a destructuring class and a shiatsu session that serves as preparation for further arenas where relationship and communication is significant. The receiver's journey from experiencing the surface of the body with awareness of fight/flight reactions and all the emotions, images and memories inherent in that touch to the transitional choice-making phase of breathing into experience that leads to relaxation and further revelation and release of an inner world, where new insights and choices can be discovered, provides a learning modality that underscores both the Voicework and shiatsu. In this way, the receiver is primed to extend this learning modality to the outer world and theoretically this could apply to the world of one's life off or on stage.

The giver's journey is equally informative. The giver is further developed through the use of the hands and fingers that learn to read the story of the body. The alignment of the hands, the skin and the nervous system create a thoroughfare of exchange that cultivates an appreciation of the shifts and messages "in the more subtle energy systems" (Goodman, author's note). The use of the hands and particularly the thumb are viewed as an endowment that grants humanity. Goodman draws a connection between shiatsu and the yogic chakra system when he asserts, " How we use our hands shows what's in our hearts. In terms of energy, the heart represents the balancing center or *chakra*, between the base of physical energies of the sacrum and abdomen, which are connected with intuition, and the mental consciousness center of the mid-brain" (5). Goodman is referring to the integration function of the heart chakra, as the transitional point between lower and higher selves, where animal intuition joins the rational powers of the mind. The giver, through touch, is granted the opportunity of integral understanding that comes through balancing the action of pressure with the receptivity of feeling:

> In order to give someone shiatsu, we need to have empathy for what that person feels. We must be able to experience what it is like to be in their body and to have their mind. While giving treatment we are asking ourselves, 'Where is their pain, their emptiness, their sorrow? Where is their joy, strength and aspiration? What is their life experience?' We need to feel these things as if they were our own" (Goodman 38).

Furthering the chakra correlation, the first chakra's essence is revealed in the survival fight/flight urge involved in the initial contact with the skin, and the second chakra surfaces in dominance when stress gives way to pleasure. Another master shiatsu practitioner, Reuho Yamada, supports this idea when he states: "Human energy is sexual in essence, but in shiatsu that energy melts into a more general ecstatic feeling. Ooooo, feels good. That's all. Sometimes I call my shiatsu Tantric Zen" (Schultz, ed. 196). In shiatsu, orgastic potency is transmuted towards the higher chakras of compassion, expression and insight. By utilizing the shiatsu method, Fitzmaurice Voicework finds a direct access for release of energy through the 5th chakra that corresponds to creativity and vocal production.

OVERVIEW

Shiatsu is readily assimilated into the Voicework. Its theories are generally porous and conversant. Shiatsu is priming the actor through touch toward self-understanding and self-integrative processes. Nevertheless, shiatsu is primarily a therapeutic modality and nonperformative. Also, the shiatsu configuration of doctor/patient in some ways reconstitutes a return to an arrangement that Alexander Lowen diverged from with the introduction of bioenergetics and the physical mobilization that it demanded of the patient. As such, shiatsu remains, even when integrated into the Voicework, as an adjunct to the more active engagements of the actor when tremoring and restructuring. Shiatsu is empowering, but when employed exclusively, it runs the risk of creating a dependency on the healer/teacher that the core ideology of the Voicework opposes.

The juncture between yoga and the Voicework is considerably more challenging. Fitzmaurice does not start from yoga forms, but there is clear overlap between her bioenergetic based postures and the asanas, for they are not exercises in the gymnasium sense of the word but are containers for expanding self awareness and developing expanded consciousness. While the asanas dovetail most palpably with the destructuring phase, the chakra system, because it is ordering, finds compatibility with the focus point and the development of organizational skills of restructuring. Yet, yoga is a paradoxical system with mystical and metaphorical dimensions that elude facile interpretation. The respected yogi, Richard Freeman considers this paradoxical turn of events fortuitous:

> ...Whenever this happens, we know that the yoga is starting to work...There's a mystery here and this is heralded by the trumpets of a paradox or a dilemma...The nature of all practice is that of a framing and a reframing. It's a dialectical process... What all these practices do, is open up the core of our body, the core of our heart, the roots of our navel, that which is hidden deep down inside at the center of this sacred soma...Our yoga practice is the microcosm of our whole life...We are finding out those core patterns, that underlying program that influences the whole tapestry of our existence (Yoga Matrix, Audio CD 1, track 11).

In spite of very compelling common ground as systems that develop human growth potential, one must acknowledge that, ultimately, yoga leads to stillness and silence in complete contrast to the more active orientation of the Voicework. Yoga moves one through transcendence to an exalted state of separation from the material world and yet paradoxically, because of its cosmic underpinning, that state is in the here and now. In the Voicework, one is grounded in the here and now with no separation from the material world or the body even when making cosmic connections.

It is fascinating to examine the reconcilable and irreconcilable differences between these approaches for promoting human growth and creativity. As psychophysical technologies leading to union, they all query and conjoin opposites whether they be will and surrender, destructuring and restructuring or the blended convergence between chaos and clarity. In spite of the distinctions, these are all systems of recovery, inner journey and transformation, and while it is not required that the actor does yoga nor shiatsu, these methods of self-study can be mutually supportive of further unfolding potentials in life and art.

CHAPTER FOUR:
CREATIVE CHAOS IN FITZMAURICE VOICEWORK

CHAOS THEORY

The paradoxical definition for chaos given in 1986 by the Royal Academy in London was "stochastic behavior occurring in a deterministic system"(Stewart 12). The paradox lies in the fact that stochastic means random, and deterministic means predictable. The paradox is resolved through the observation that chaos self-organizes into order (Prigogine 141). If classical physics is a system that yields determined predictions and quantum mechanics is the study of probabilities, then chaos, because of its inherent self-organizing process, hypothetically and potentially leads to a reconciliation of the tensions between old and new science. According to Ian Percival, "The theory of deterministic chaos mixes determinism and probability in a totally unexpected way" (15). On a parallel path, Fitzmaurice combines the traditional instructions of classical Western voice training with the esoteric study of energy systems, such as chakras and meridians, in quest of a more dynamic, expressive, present actor. In her explorations, she encountered, as did the quantum physicists, a world of probabilities, and she realized that the inner world and the links to it–breath and mind–have diverse applications.

The task she set for herself was to develop a system that would harmonize with the esoteric Eastern paths but channel those energies in the pragmatic ways of actor training. In the foreword to Chaos, Creativity and Cosmic Consciousness, Jean Houston writes, "We live in chaos, which we may have created in order to hasten our own meeting with ourselves – that is to blow down the old structures that no longer sustain us" (Sheldrake, McKenna, and Abraham xv). This apt citation justifies the model for Fitzmaurice Voicework, which is a *magnum opus* in the alchemical sense of transformation, whereby chaos is both consciously and unconsciously created as a learning modality toward fuller self-knowledge in the service of broader creativity. This is psycho-spiritual alchemy that aligns with Jungian theories of transformation. C. G. Jung cites many alchemists to draw the conclusion that the alchemical process was not only material but psychological, "It should now be sufficiently clear that from its earliest days alchemy had a double face: on the one hand the practical chemical work in the laboratory, on the other a psychological process, in part consciously psychic, in part unconsciously projected and seen in the various transformations of matter" (270). John Conger gives a summation of Jung's alchemical process when he writes, "The work of alchemy was to bring about the union of opposites, as in the Eastern concept of Atman and Tao. The third stage unites the adept with the unus mundus, psychologically understood as a synthesis of the conscious with the unconscious" (153). This idea resonates with the goal of the Fitzmaurice restructured actor toward more holistic expression. But while the alchemical process starts with the *prima materia,* often characterized as chaos in its aspect as the *massa confusa* (Jung 340), Fitzmaurice starts from the notion of a kind of chaos that is not confusion but a purposeful interweave of both right and left brain behaviors that enrich creative choice-making. This reframing away from confusion suggests a permissive approach to the creative psyche that does not stigmatize its complexities. Breath acts as a kind of connective tissue in providing both intrinsic and extrinsic links that support the vocal expression of these rich, human complex thoughts. Her method heals the post Cartesian mind/body split through harmonizing the autonomic nervous system with the central nervous system while preserving the innate density of the experience that is expressed. The diaphragm, as a site of both striated and nonstriated muscle, becomes the symbol of this harmony through her foundational work on the breath. The unique theoretical ingredient of her work is that it embraces the "fight or flight" mechanism rather than banishing the fear it generates. In this way, not by banishing fear but by utilizing it, she claims to heighten vocal expression. As a Fitzmaurice trained actor, one wants to manage one's resources and sustain consistency and skill in performance, but this expertise is arrived at through exploring uncertainties rather than suppressing or denying them. In this way, the Voicework interweaves with a mysterious element of chaos theory as stated by Briggs and Peat, "Chaotic systems lie beyond all our attempts to predict, manipulate, and control them. Chaos suggests that instead of resisting life's uncertainties, we should embrace them" (Lessons 8).

METAPHOR AND SYNCHRONICITY

What I propose in this chapter is a synaptic study of a metaphoric nature between Fitzmaurice Voicework and chaos theory. It is important to make this clarification since not all scientists agree on the definition of deterministic chaos, and many of them, such as Stephen Kellert (78), would argue that a metaphorical or metaphysical perspective of the theory corrupts the scientific constructs that inform it. It can also be argued that such narrowing of perspective is the result of a particular kind of "westernized" logic that is a by-product of exclusive insularity. Swami Ajaya offers an alternative to the "reductive mode of thought" that is more supportive of a global village by pointing out that "Eastern philosophy" looks for mutually enriching and complementary dynamics between seeming opposites (Psychology 42). In addition, often when the arts are juxtaposed with the sciences, a hierarchical relationship ensues with science on top. Such dialogues contain what Bohm and Peat identify as a "subliminal infrastructure of tacit ideas"(39). They are referring to paradigms inherent in the scientific community reflective of rigid thinking, but the same kind of silent conspiracy can be found in conversational formats when the humanities are linked to and borrow from a scientific context. In such hierarchical transactions, the tendency is to valorize the sciences and to devalue the arts. While a hierarchical configuration may be valid and most efficient for a closed system of study, a more flexible structure is needed in cross-disciplinary discussions, such as the one offered in this chapter.

Numerous fields of study, heretofore considered antithetical to the "hard" sciences, have appropriated chaos theory. This inclusive, global potential has infiltrated a variety of non-strictly scientific studies from economics to Hollywood special effects. Clearly, chaos theory has gained authority in such arenas, but, as Fritjof Capra attests in the Tao of Physics through numerous citations of eminent scientists, the Eastern mystics got there first (18). Scientists are now admitting, therefore, that this so-called new wave of physics is really only in process of catching up to the concepts of ancient Eastern cosmology. Yet as Briggs and Peat clarify, this is not a process of mere replication as much as it is of new generation:

> Paradoxically, the insights of the newest science share the vision of the world presented in many of the world's oldest indigenous and spiritual traditions. This doesn't mean that chaos theory is about to return us to some mythic golden age or idealized culture, but it does mean that the enduring insights of these cultures will help us elaborate the metaphor of chaos and high-light the way chaos reenvisions ancient wisdom in a brand-new form relevant for our high tech, high-octane, cyber-saturated age (Lessons 7).

In such complex exchanges of ideas between cultures, hierarchy as a model is crumbling. The impact of Eastern mystical modalities on the West has had a leveling effect that has pervaded dialogical comparisons. When the relationship is so porous and fluid, alternative methods of discussion must be sought.

This chapter does not attempt to present a definitive summation of a scientific theory. Instead, it looks for engaging parallels from science to further illuminate a field of voice training. Following Julian Jayne's dissection of metaphor, Fitzmaurice Voicework is the *metaphrand,* and chaos theory is the *metaphier,* where the former is "the thing to be described", and the latter is "the thing or relation used to elucidate it" (48). I posit that it is possible to offer such a metaphorical study when this authority is put in a context that admits both the Voicework and chaos theories' constructs recover ancient perceptions. As Michael Berry notes, " Nowadays the 'chaology' of classical mechanics is an intensively active area of research – chaology is a revival of a term used by theologians two centuries ago to mean the study of what existed before the Creation" (185-6). One can correspondingly argue that Fitzmaurice Voicework is also a process of recovery in offering the actor the potential for reconnection with vital energies, ideas and imagination prior to creativity through vocal expression. In support of clarifying this parallel, one can turn to Briggs and Peat who distinguish active from passive chaos, "Mythic chaos had been 'the first of all things' out of which bloomed forms and life. The passive chaos of entropy was the reverse. It was what happened when forms and systems ran down or ran out of the energy that had bound them together" (Mirror 22). In Fitzmaurice Voicework I will not be looking at dissipative but creative, active chaos. Fitzmaurice Voicework has underpinnings in this context, since destructuring is in the service of and precedes structural creation. Scientific chaos theory provides the primary dialogue of this essay, but the metaphoric approach affords other reflections too that intersect with mythic chaos. For example, I will also briefly consider chaos in shamanism and spirit possession as possible dialogic interplays with Fitzmaurice actor training.

Another connective underpinning is that both Fitzmaurice Voicework and chaos theory have common ties to Eastern philosophy that create mutual meeting points. Furthermore, both chaos theory and Fitzmaurice Voicework provide us with a rich and compelling vocabulary. It is important to acknowledge, however, that Fitzmaurice arrived at a technology and terminology independent of chaos theory in her pursuit of a comprehensive system of voice training. It is moreover significant to this kind of dialogue to acknowledge that synchronicity plays a part, for in the 1960's when Edward Lorenz was making his discovery known as the "butterfly effect", that would prove to be foundational to the new science of chaos, Fitzmaurice was conducting her own experiments researching energy in the body and discovering how an induced tremor was fundamental to her system of voice. Peat puts this synchronic phenomena in a possible context, giving shared time events deeper harmonic overtones, when he writes, "Synchronicities are therefore often associated with periods of transformation; for example, births, deaths, falling in love, psychotherapy, intense creative work, and even a change of profession. It is as if this internal restructuring produces external resonances or as if a burst of 'mental energy' is propagated outward into the physical world" (27). Following this logic, there is an energetic connection between events apparently separated by space but linked by time.

It is interesting to muse about the fact that the Newtonian clockwork universe synchronized with the philosopher Denis Diderot's evaluation of the accomplished actor as a marionette in The Paradox of Acting: " a great actor is also a most ingenious puppet, and his strings are held by the poet, who at each line indicates the true form he must take" (46). Joseph Roach, who tracks the science/art parallel in The Player's Passion, concludes that Diderot "discovered a perfect acting machine" in David Garrick because of what he describes as his automaton-like alterations of expression (152). Synchronicity may have contributed to Garrick's brilliant success in an age that exalted the machine over nature. By comparison, Fitzmaurice grew up in a world beyond quantum physics that had already interrogated determinism, questioned the antagonistic relationship formed by science's subjugation of nature and was moving in some circles toward new paradigms that sought to restore order through chaos. While her work, therefore, may be seen as merely reflective of her time, there is an alternative perspective that could view it as springing from the same energy that shaped the time and co-creative with other events through active participation.

FITZMAURICE VOICEWORK REVISITED

Before further advancing this discussion, I will review the two phases of Fitzmaurice voice practice. The first phase, destructuring, is comprised of a series of exercises that stimulate and support the actor's exploration of spontaneous impulses. Destructuring operates by moving the actor through a sequence of semi-stressful positions that are related to yoga asanas and informed by Alexander Lowen's adaptation of Reichian therapy–bioenergetics. The exercises are intended to bring the actor in contact with the autonomic nervous system. These positions permit an energy flow in the body that Fitzmaurice calls "tremoring". It is important to distinguish tremoring from shaking; the former considered an involuntary reaction, while the latter implies active intention. The tremors are vibratory, quivering motions that affect the breathing and also act as a diagnostic tool that allows for consciousness of where there is flow of energy and where there are blocks. Often where the tremor stops, consciousness stops. Fitzmaurice aims for what she identifies as "global breathing"–the sense of the breath going all through the body. As the tremor influences breathing it also influences the voice. The tremor acts like a current and sensitizes the body to the flow of vibration. The premise is that vocal resonance will follow where the breath goes, so as the tremor opens up the whole physical field, it also carves a path for sound flow. The tremoring energy encourages the possibility that sound vibration will therefore deeply penetrate the whole body.

The actor practices the art of releasing unmanaged sound or what Fitzmaurice calls "fluffy sound". This is a breathy sound using minimal activation of the vocal folds in order to keep the neck muscles loose. The idea is to allow the breath and sound to occur as a release and reflection of what's going on in the body. Destructuring affects the body as well as vocal organization, inviting greater range, resonance, and fluidity of thought with emotional release.

The second phase, restructuring is the complementary phase that follows destructuring. This phase promotes the reconnection with the central nervous system through isolation and synergistic use of the intercostals and the transversalis abdominis but not the rectus abdominis or the abdominal obliques for improved vocal function. Restructuring represents the more Western orientation of the work, including rib swings and a physiological approach to breath and sound production. Restructuring includes speech and also reifies a more Eastern orientation through the imagined "focus-line" that starts at the navel, travels down to the basin of the pelvis and moves up parallel to the spine and out through the third eye towards the listener. The focus-line involves synthesizing the interiority discovered in destructuring with the conscious intent to communicate.

CONSCIOUSNESS

Fitzmaurice claims that in stimulating the fight/flight mechanism via tremoring, the actor attains alpha states similar to those reached in meditation. Indeed, in the time-altered world of destructuring, the brain may continue to decompress and attain theta states too. Keith Floyd describes this magical alteration through the eyes of a meditator, "He finds his mind flooded with creative insights, as if it has established direct contact with every mind that has ever been or ever will be. It could almost be described as a dimension of awareness beyond space and time. His consciousness is expanding and he feels himself at the threshold of what has been called Cosmic Consciousness" (49). At oneness with Cosmic Consciousness occurs at the theta level where time is spaced out. This mind opening for the Fitzmaurice trained actor to universal consciousness is most tangible through inspiration, which is literally the liberated movement of the breath. It is through the physical approach of destructured breathing that the mind is encountered. It is in the doing the prescribed exercises that the understanding happens. By altering the body, one alters the mind, and it is through this expanded, porous consciousness that one is able to receive character insights for vocal expression when acting.

Fitzmaurice utilizes the proprioceptive mechanism–that part of the nervous system that governs self-perception–in order to enhance awareness of the body. Mabel Elsworth Todd defines proprioceptive in her book on movement, The Thinking Body:

> But the body possesses the power of reacting to gravity, inertia and momentum, the primary forces of the physical world, by means of that part of the nervous system known as proprioceptive or 'perceiving of self,' as distinguished from the exteroceptive mechanisms by which the outer world is perceived.

> The proprioceptive sensations, also called 'organic,' are grouped, according to their origins in various parts of the organism, into three general types: the 'feeling of movement,', in all skeletal and muscular structures, called kinesthesia; the feeling of position in space, derived from organs in the inner ear and known as labyrinthine; and miscellaneous impressions from various internal organs, as of digestion and excretion, called viscera.

> Altogether, the proprioceptive system, acting in conjunction with all the outer senses, serves to guide our total reaction to the outside world in terms of motion toward or away from particular objects,

and give us our ideas of space and time. More than any other factor the proprioceptive system is responsible for the appearance of the individual as an organized unit when he is moving about (p. 26-7).

In addition to developing a fine-tuned sense of the body in space, this work involves the development of interoception–an awareness of the body's internal state. The tremoring doesn't just move in the skeletal muscles; it moves in the organs as well. By bringing the mind into the body, both are experienced as energy with a flowing quality that permits dialogue, transmission and merger between the two. This fluid quality of mind and body create an internal terrain where choice and change become tangible. The tremoring body not only moves physical energy, but there is also a corresponding upheaval of consciousness as the mind unleashes thoughts, images and inner voices that, through the agency of the breath, extend beyond the borders of the head and flood the body. In this way, thoughts become physical and visceral. A large part of the destructuring work is to disrupt, through chaos, patterns of holding in muscle and mind in order to change self-perception.

Chaos occurs when the energy elicited through tremoring encounters a habitually held region of the body. The breathing becomes chaotic and the body/mind are flooded with associations to tremors such as shivering, nervousness, sexual release, muscle fatigue, anger and perhaps most appropriately to the actor, stage fright. Tremoring may induce these emotions that are appropriate for this transformational work aligning with Briggs and Peat's assessment when they observe, "Artists, healers, and those undergoing life changes open up to the uncertainties, accessing degrees of freedom that can spur new self-organization" (Lessons 22). The tremor is evoking a primal survival response that tends to make respiration deeper and raises the internal body temperature. Destructuring, therefore, reconnects the actor with primal body intelligence, allowing for a more responsive, alert system of breathing and sounding. Since there is an emotional association with "fight or flight" instincts, the potential increases for more sensitized textured responses. Destructuring disorganizes mind/body habits on the premise that there is innate wisdom in the actor's psyche; that "deeper authenticity" (Lessons 20) will be uncovered which enhances the actor's creative work.

DARK MATTER

These "fight or flight" instincts are often buried in the unconscious of a wounded, fragmented psyche. Fitzmaurice re-frames wounds as a positive structuring of protection that functioned historically as an intelligent reaction to stressful conditions. But as the wound becomes buried, it serves another function holding the possibility for healing and renewal. Fitzmaurice states, "the wound and the protection system is gold because you remember yourself. It's a gift. More than a personal journey, it becomes a gift to the world, bringing yourself to a barrier and walking through it" (5th Teacher Certification Program 15 Jan. 2005). According to Fitzmaurice, "Shit is fertile – and your life depends on getting rid of your shit" (5th Teacher Training). It is the inner world of dark shit that provides both the enrichment for creativity as well as the toxic interior that constipates the actor if not identified and released. The dark interior can either be constructive or destructive depending on the mind's relationship to it. It reinforces the actor's resourcefulness to recognize its prevalence and form an ally relationship with this dark interior. There is a reflection in the cosmos that Sheldrake points to:

> I think a factor that changes everything is the discovery of dark matter – the fact that 90 to 99 percent of the matter in the universe is utterly unknown to us. This recent discovery effectively tells us that the cosmos has a kind of unconscious, a dark realm that condition the formation and shapes of the galaxies, their interaction, and everything that's going on within them (Sheldrake, McKenna, and Abraham 16-17).

In the human microcosm, Fitzmaurice assists actors in working around their edges and sometimes going beyond their boundaries through tremoring to contact their dark matter. Briggs and Peat draw from the therapeutic tradition that contains potential for the creative process when they write:

> The history of the world's religions is full of stories about mystics and sages who spent time in the 'wilderness' – either literally or through some 'dark night of the soul' and inner chaos. Healing of mind and body in many traditional societies involves a descent into darkness, chaos and death. Greek healers encouraged 'incubation,' in which a sick individual was required to sleep and dream. Using ceremonies designed to loosen the grip of the conscious ego,

the sick person was encouraged to let go of the familiar structures of his life and enter the dark world of the gods and underground forces. By letting go of the consensual structures, a creative self-reorganization became possible (Lessons 22).

Metaphors of the dark world permeate the modality of destructuring, but the actor's descent into this inner void of chaos is not a sleep induced state as much as a relaxed alertness.

CHAOS INTO FLOW

Giving space to the irrational becomes a means of growth and insight as de-rigidified patterns transform into creative energy. The nature of the tremor is paradoxical with its contradictory energy flows. The contradictions occur in the multiplicity of impulses that bombard the actor's psychophysical awareness. Contradictions encountered through tremoring contain the solution and, in this sense, is comparable to the Zen koan described by Capra: "Once the solution is found, the koan ceases to be paradoxical and becomes a profoundly meaningful statement made from the state of consciousness which it has helped to awaken" (49). Tremoring, too, is a way to consciousness, to direct insight; literally seeing in through a process of de-armoring that uncovers the core of innate information about the self. The juxtaposition of flow with obstruction leads to chaotic natural behavior such as observed in whirlpools or the weather. The tremor serves as a "butterfly effect", disturbing the mundane, armored persona by throwing it into a fragmented world of rough edges where mind and body move toward union. The chaotic trajectory of the tremoring body/mind is in a perpetual state of butterfly effects where each moment is a perturbation of initial conditions. The butterfly effect is metaphoric for the smallest of alterations, having a profound and far reaching impact. It is represented by the smallest of tremors in an actor positioned in a physical position that challenges familiarity. These positions adapted from yoga asanas and bioenergetics is designed to de-stabilize the actor in pursuit of more creative options. Briggs and Peat note that: "Biological systems remain stable by damping most small effects except in those areas of behavior where a high degree of flexibility and creativity is required" (Mirror 145). The human dynamical system is open, and each tremoring shift has many bifurcations. This inner journey reveals what Michael Talbot calls "universes within universes" (39). Like the subatomic world, the interior landscape explored through tremoring is a place of probabilities and potentials.

The difficulty encountered in approaching these potentials is due to investment in patterns of bracing, which have significant application to survival on the mundane level of existence but which tend to limit the resources required of the actor in the heightened realm of theater. Fitzmaurice's antidote to bracing is to stimulate energy flow both in the body and mind. Edward Lorenz, forefather of chaos theory, was investigating fluid flow when he discovered the butterfly effect (Lorenz 13), as was Wilhelm Reich when he arrived at his cosmic connection. It is interesting to note that the ancient systems had a long head start in observation of fluids, as noted in the *Tao Te Ching*: "Nothing in the world is as soft and yielding as water. Yet for dissolving the hard and inflexible, nothing can surpass it" (Mitchell 78). Bohm and Peat provide a rationale for the necessity of flow: "Rigidly fixed ideas similarly obstruct the flowing of the 'stream' in the space of the mind. To free this flow therefore requires the removal of the obstruction" (225). The obstructive knots for an actor are in the form of tension, and it is in keeping within this mystical, paradoxical framework to discover that in Fitzmaurice Voicework, the element employed to resolve a congested mass of matter is the unsubstantial air that we breathe. Fitzmaurice views the breath as a power source. Its energetics allows it to traverse physical and mental barriers.

FRACTALS

The intention is to delve below the surface to stimulate subterranean life flow through tremors in order to unearth a myriad of potentials that ultimately determine vocal expression. The geological metaphor dovetails with geometry in the concept of *fractals*. This term is used in physics to describe non-Euclidean geometric shapes that are self-similar on any scale. Benoit Mandelbrot gave science this term:

> I coined the word fractal in 1975 from the Latin *fractus*, which describes a broken stone – broken up and irregular. Fractals are geometrical shapes that, contrary to those of Euclid, are not regular at all. First, they are irregular all over. Secondly, they have the same degree of irregularity on all scales. A fractal object looks the same when examined from far away or nearby – it is self similar" (123-4).

Fractals occur in nature and can be seen in the irregular shapes of coastlines, rocks, trees and broccoli. It is the natural fractal rather than the mathematical one with which Fitzmaurice Voicework aligns. Briggs and Peat make a distinction when they write:

> Mathematical fractals are impressive, but after repeated viewing, the freshness of one of these objects fades. This doesn't happen with the creations of nature, which emerge out of a holistic chaotic process whereby countless 'parts' are subtly interconnected – true chaos as opposed to mathematical simulation produced by repeating algorithm. Consequently, natural fractals have an individuality, spontaneity, depth, and quality of mystery that no algorithm – even a nonlinear one – can reproduce (<u>Lessons</u> 117-8).

The root of the word, which means to break, gives us the words *fracture* and *fragment*. In his definition Gleick observes, "In the end, the word *fractal* came to stand for a way of describing, calculating, and thinking about shapes that are irregular and fragmented, jagged and broken-up – shapes from the crystalline curves of snowflakes to the discontinuous dusts of galaxies" (113-4). The lungs are fractal space with their dense network of branching, bifurcating bronchioles and honeycomb alveoli. The very character of thought seems to harmonize with chaotic constructs of the natural environment. This point is corroborated by Gleick: "Such models seemed to have the right features: points of stability mixed with instability, and regions with changeable boundaries. Their fractal structure offered the kind of infinitely self-referential quality that seems so central to the mind's abilty to bloom with ideas, decisions, emotions, and all other artifacts of consciousness" (299). Thus, Fitzmaurice Voicework enters a fractal domain with exercises that honor, nurture and support the native chaos of the human psyche and body. Tremoring takes its cues from the fractal environment. Tremoring offers the actor an excursion into a fractal landscape that is explored rather than suppressed or arranged. Clues to character are embodied in fractal structures that contain a "study of an evolutionary process" (Peak and Frame 101) with a density of information. Metaphorically, fractals resonate with monsters. Briggs and Peat justify this conclusion when they write, "When nineteenth-century mathematicians discovered what are now called fractal shapes (the mathematical versions), they called them 'monsters' and 'pathological'. This suggests our profound investment in idealized forms, an investment rampant in much of modern culture" (<u>Lessons</u> 112).

Through her exercise called "Monsters", Fitzmaurice assists the actor in uncovering the borderlands of humanity in order to infuse the psyche and body with a primal understanding contained in the richness of "otherness". This exploration informs the depth of availability and selection for far- from-equilibrium creative choices, those choices that the actor undertakes outside of one's comfort zone in realizing character. Her work has moved the actor away from the prescribed pear shape tones of the nineteenth- century toward the complexity of vocal expression in the age of chaos.

ATTRACTORS

Another term used in chaos theory that finds application in Fitzmaurice Voicework is attractor. According to Ian Stewart, an attractor "in general dynamical systems...is defined to be... whatever it settles down to!"(99). The attractor is a point or cycle that the system converges on. Strange attractors are specific to chaotic systems when the pattern settled down to is unpredictable but within a limited boundary. This paradox is at the heart of chaos theory in describing chaotic behavior within a definable spatial frame. " The motion on a strange attractor has," what David Ruelle calls, "sensitive dependence on initial conditions" (64). In Fitzmaurice Voicework, centers of energy, such as chakras, function as attractors while initial conditions set up through tremoring cause a pattern of behavior that follows the unpredictable path of a strange attractor. Tremoring waves are congruous with turbulence, but there is "a subtle form of order" (Mirror 45) intrinsic to the chaotic process. Briggs and Peat state: "It turns out that there is nothing new about the strange attractor. Its presence had merely been hidden from us under another name – turbulence" (Mirror 45). Strange attractors are fractal both in the irregularity of the tremoring rhythm as well as the self-similarity. Self-similar does not mean self-identical, and each tremoring wave has its own identity but still is energetically similar to other tremors. In this way, the actor in destructuring may run a gamut from small to large tremors without losing the psycho-emotional intensity that links them.

Self-similarity permits a metaphoric bond between tremors that opens up kaleidoscopic reflections. The dark destructured world creates many mirrors that hold potential insight for the actor exploring this fractal domain. Briggs and Peat provide a stimulating analogy when they posit, "The notion of vortices within vortices ad infinitum suggests that systems close to turbulence will look similar to themselves at smaller and smaller scales – suggesting again that the strange attractor of turbulence is a mirror- world" (Mirror 49). Part of the excitement, fear and or pleasure elicited through tremoring is that it opens up a world of probabilities and potentials. Prior to the choice- making of structuring, the destructured chaotic terrain is full of playful indecision. It is a fertile ground for creativity. This does not mean that choice is not present in tremoring. Instead what is happening is a multiplicity of micro-events, where choices are perpetually emerging and the actor is fine-tuning awareness moment to moment as choices well up. The rapid fluctuations of tremors create a paradoxical environment as contrasting and contradictory thoughts, images and emotions flow up from the actor's well of memory and imagination. It is a constantly bifurcating world. Schisms may occur in the encounter between a holding pattern and the energy below it that is held, and, within that energy, there may be a continuum of dialogues as new insights and impulses push the journey of exploration forward toward expression.

Tremoring impulses may be both repetitive in their modus operandi but very contradictory in the information that they contain. Instead of leading to breakdown this paradoxical environment can lead to growth. Briggs and Peat observe:

> For a computer iterative paradoxes lead to chaos. For human beings they are said to have the opposite power – leading to creative insight or even enlightenment. In mystical systems like Zen Buddhism, self-looping koans supposedly set the mind of the student oscillating in a way that creates the conditions for it to bubble free into a new point of view (or a viewless point)" (Mirror 67).

Unlike a computer faced with paradoxical iterative information, actors presented with the tremoring of Fitzmaurice Voicework enter chaos not as an end point but as an entrance towards growth. Fitzmaurice Voicework puts the actor in semi-stressful positions that provide this information in a shifting ground for transformation.

Paradoxically, a certain amount of stress leads to growth in human dynamical systems, and there is some scientific evidence to support this. In a study suggesting that stress provoked resiliency is beneficial, the authors note:

> The conventional wisdom in medicine holds that disease and aging arise from stress on an otherwise orderly and machinelike system – that the stress decreased order by provoking erratic responses or by upsetting the body's normal periodic rhythms. In the past five years or so we and our colleagues have discovered that the heart and

146

other physiological systems may behave most erratically when they are young and healthy. Counterintutitively, increasingly regular behavior sometimes accompanies ageing and disease" (Goldberger, Rigney, and West 42-3).

For far from equilibrium systems, like a tremoring body in a semi-stressful position, instability can lead to transformation and to more evolved modes of thinking, behaving and sounding. Briggs and Peat present an insight that supports the chaos of tremoring when they state: "At its bifurcation points, the system undergoing flux is, in effect, being offered a 'choice' of orders. The internal feedback of some of the choices is so complex that there is a virtual infinity of degrees of freedom. In other words the order of the choice is so high that it is chaos" (Mirror 143). Chaos, therefore, is not so much disorder as it is complicated order or "a very subtle form of order" (Mirror 181). This order, below the appearance of chaos, is the organizing principle that Fitzmaurice Voicework seeks to recover.

Bifurcations also contain the notion of split, and this plays into the kinds of behavior that is altered into dualities that provide the basis for study of personality in psychotherapeutic disciplines. For this reason Fitzmaurice's system can be adapted to a healing modality, although she chooses to work with actors in the theatrical arena with a clear focus on the craft of heightened communication. For the actor there is also the insight that comes through understanding bifurcations in terms of character adjustments, and tremoring can provide a basis for exploring how a character makes choices that reflect as patterns of holding and action. The actor's own psyche, if present in these explorations, enrich and deepen the flow of insight into character by tapping into a mutual humanity. Tremoring can instantly convert to the experience of pleasure or pain as personal wounds or habits are elicited in the wake of such energetic flow. Briggs and Peat note that, "Systems are also highly sensitive near those places that are crystallized 'memory' of past bifurcations" (Mirror 145). When moving to characterization, in the chaotic context, the chakra system becomes an ordering system assisting in arranging the waves of energetic flow, because they are internal focus points. The heart chakra, for example, is a place of change where the lower elements transmute to the higher elements. In traditional yogic philosophy, a focus of energy here elicits compassion for others, and it is therefore important to incorporate this center into the shift from inner world to outer and from self to other. It becomes a launch point for communication that provides a prompt for restructured breathing.

In the cosmic realm there are two types of attractors: one that pulls us toward our destiny and another that drives us to create our destiny. In Fitzmaurice Voicework, the goal is to align the two so that the attractors converge on the goal of a restructured dynamically charged resonant capable actor's instrument. Entering the training arena, however, actors bring attractors with them that are social, cultural, and psychological constructs that have influence on self-perception and restrict the possibility of a holistic trajectory towards their goal. In Fitzmaurice Voicework the instability of the tremor is metaphoric for the interrogation of the self. Through that upheaval, tremors unearth images that both synergistically nourish and contradict those established attractors that reside in the actor's body/mind. This transitional phase equates with Stanley Keleman's "middle ground", where he states, "Learning to live in its creative sea, one experiences the pull of the past and the thrust toward the future" (79). The images arrived at through tremoring act as attractors themselves in the chaotic void of destructuring, pulling new energy and insights with them. Such stimulated visualizations can birth new self-imagery through a deeper and expanded physical and mental consciousness. The synthesis between following one's destiny and creating one's reality can function dialogically in the dark world of tremors. The womb of chaos provides a multiplicity of information that prepares the actor for the next phase, restructuring, where choice-making becomes significant.

TRANSITIONS

The Voicework instructs the actor to live within the gaps between perceived dualities of chaos and order through the breath. Fitzmaurice Voicework is an ongoing process perhaps without an omega point, because it embraces the dynamics of change and chaos with choice and focus. These transitions and shift stages all represent energetic phases where cyclical yin and yang transmute into each other. At these intersections, the actor has the opportunity of encountering self and driving out restrictive habits. Chaos happens in that synaptic moment of encounter, and the breath/sound/ movement repetitions are never identical but contain a holographic similarity, each encounter moment containing the kernel of the whole self within it. If chaos is not confusion, and if the images it unleashes as the actor tremors are not random, then creativity is purposeful. Chaos is dynamic; it causes structure. The form is a product of chaos and not antithetical to it. Therefore, as Keleman notes, "Every organizing process has a middle phase where organization is minimal. It is, in fact, embryogenesis, similar to the process whereby the organs are formed before the organism becomes human" (78). Thus according to Fitzmaurice, " Destructuring long enough instantly arranges into structuring" (5th Teacher Certification Program 15 Jan. 2005), or as Sheldrake remarks, in seeking an alternative to Platonic pre-formed higher reality where everything on earth is a mimesis or else random creativity, "I'm trying to look at a third possibility in which imagination, instead of emerging from the light of the future or from a kind of Platonic mind, may emerge from something more like the unconscious mind –coming into light from darkness" (9-10). This emanation of light from darkness resonates with Shamanism and suggests a kinship between the shaman and the actor. While basic differences between the two must be acknowledged, the actor in the destructured phase of Fitzmaurice Voicework becomes adept at seeing in the dark, in this way taking on a shamanic identity, and in the restructuring phase harmonizes with the hero bringing the dark into light described by Joseph Campbell (217).

CHAOS IN FITZMAURICE VOICEWORK AND SHAMANISM

The metaphors of shamanism may overlap with Fitzmaurice Voicework, but it is important to the understanding of her process to keep them distinct. Yet an actor's imagination might be further stimulated by some of the terminology from other disciplines that interrogate and illuminate the Voicework. Both disciplines employ creative chaos and move toward union and transformation. But while observing parallels, it is necessary to remember that Fitzmaurice is largely a system of communication geared toward the pragmatic needs of the performing actor. Eliade equates shamanism with a "technique of ecstasy" in his classic book on the subject (4). Ecstasy literally means a being out of its place. But Eliade qualifies when he writes, "Hence any ecstatic cannot be considered a shaman. The shaman specializes in a trance during which his soul is believed to leave his body and ascend to the sky or descend to the underworld" (5). Does Fitzmaurice Voicework through tremoring qualify as a technique of ecstasy? The borders blur if one thinks of shamans as the mediators between people and their gods, for an actor in training may be groomed to accomplish something similar between the audience and their gods or demons. Entering a dark interior via tremoring positions the actor to bring back potentially healing insights from the underworld of the unconscious as well as inspirational messages from the cosmic consciousness. The "two-fold initiation – ecstatic and didactic – that transforms the candidate from a possible neurotic into a shaman is recognized by his particular society" (Eliade 14) may also apply in Fitzmaurice training, since the skill required by the student is to allow the voice to serve as a medium of insights while not becoming totally consumed to the point of incapacitation by the psycho-physical releases that are engendered. Shamanism can be viewed within the matrix of the hero's journey as drawn by Joseph Campbell from the call to adventure, initiation, trial and return that may also parallel an actor's quest in training, in preparing, or in performing a role (245).

However, if one sees training as initiatory and subscribes to Eliade's three phases: suffering, death and resurrection, the metaphorical link to Fitzmaurice Voicework may be pushed too far. The literal call to vocation of the shaman is as a healer and retriever of the human soul, and it is important to focus on this curative aspect of shamanism. While performance may have a healing effect through the much discussed Aristotelian concept of catharsis, and while the actor in training may have therapeutic results for the student, Fitzmaurice does not see her work in terms of therapy as the ultimate goal. Instead, the pragmatic function of communication and interpretation of text prevails over spiritual regeneration, which may be a by-product but not the direct pursuit. The text and voice may be informed by spiritual or psycho-emotional epiphanies, but it is the play of communication that is the trajectory.

Then there is the question of trance, which has several meanings according to Webster's New World Dictionary and Thesaurus:

> 1) A state of altered consciousness, somewhat resembling sleep, during which voluntary movement is lost, as in hypnosis. 2) A stunned condition, daze, stupor. 3) A condition of great mental concentration or abstraction, esp. one induced by religious fervor or mysticism. 4) In spiritualistic belief, a condition in which a medium passes under the control of some external force, as for the transmission of communications from the dead during a séance (CD Rom, Macmillan Digital Publishing).

The word trance is rooted in the Latin word meaning to perish or die and relates to transit and transitions. Holger Kalweit in Shamans, Healers and Medicine Men notes, "One must suffer the disintegration of one's own system of thought in order to perceive a new world in the higher space" (4). The Voicework does create an opportunity for disintegration via destructuring, but the actor is not limited to suffering since pleasure may play a part in that process of breakdown. Relinquishing body/thought patterns can be joyously liberating. Also, in Fitzmaurice Voicework rather than the entrance of a god or foreign entity described in a trance, there is instead the connecting with the internal powers or more mythically put, the creative god within, through the stress-induced tremor. One is not possessed as much in the Voicework as possessing, acknowledging and recognizing one's own possibilities for creativity. Further, Maya Deren writes in <u>Divine Horsemen</u> that there is an essential split between the will and the body involved in possession (261), but Fitzmaurice Voicework moves in a contrastive way toward union of will, mind and body.

But does Fitzmaurice Voicework move the actor through trance to conscious synthesis? Hypothetically, the actor may start in a kind of trance where the mind and body are possessed by a myriad of thought forms impregnating from the outside and lodging in a psyche that they direct through habit. In the shifting modality of tremoring, the instilled outer world may collide with the intrinsic inner world, so that the concept of inner space is disrupted. Trance often produces spasms in the possessed, but something more willful happens in the consciously induced tremoring actor who borders on the territory of sleep states in deep relaxation but does not lose consciousness. The actor remains a witness to inner chaos, and the voice recovered is native, not alien. But to witness does not mean to split off from experiences. There is not required disassociation as in trance. There may be a desire to disassociate, but while tremoring, the actor remains alert. In fact, the shift may be from the trance-like waking state of the consciousness of narrow mundane existence to a heightened awareness within the realm of destructuring. The trance may be a start point, and there may be vital moments where the actor experiences chaotic involuntary movements, great anxiety, fear and heat, but the discipline is to stay in one's body, not to vacate it.

Yet the experience of tremoring can coincide with fear that something will be lost, as it does in shamanic ecstasy. Kalweit identifies this as ego death. He parallels this to the act of falling, which pertinent to this study, Reich discussed in some detail too. Kalweit presents some fascinating connections and divergences from the Voicework when he writes:

> In the face of mortal danger – as when one's body is in free fall – and when all means of escape within human capacity are futile, consciousness abandons itself to its fate. The fear of ego dissolution vanishes, and one's identification with his or her own life story and existence falls apart.

Once people are liberated from the crazed fears of their ego, they can adopt a more objective, emotionless standpoint. At that point they are in possession of a clear consciousness, and the activity of their thoughts intensifies to a level resembling a filmstrip running at high speed. At that time, their thoughts become a great deal more precise. They calculate the sequence of events of the accident and its outcome in advance with lightning speed, as though with a computer. They calculate their own chances of survival realistically, they run through all possible preventive reactions, and in the midst of all this they remain capable of suitable spontaneous action. Instead of confusion, their minds are filled with clarity, objectivity, and an extraordinary inner calm and seriousness. Since they undertake no unsuitable or awkward survival efforts, their bodies remain completely relaxed. Calm, composure and a feeling of peace prevail. They accommodate themselves to their fate and no longer attempt to brace themselves against the inevitable results of the fall through space (87-8).

The arrival of calm through the presentation of danger is connected to the arousal of the autonomic nervous system, to a point beyond fight or flight, where acceptance and relaxation takes over. Kalweit goes on to equate this state of falling with trance in its relinquishing of ego control. Fitzmaurice and Kalweit may be going in the same direction but the Voicework tends to support the chaotic and not diminish its importance as part of the creative journey as Kalweit does, "By contrast the more chaotic the perception and the more objects there are in the field of view, the flatter and vaguer the impression. An accident quite naturally focuses one's attention to the utmost. All shamanic consciousness techniques are aimed at narrowing perception to one-pointed conscious being" (Kalweit 90). The aim of Fitzmaurice Voicework via focus point has a similar clarity in the return back to the world of conscious communication, but the actor's clarity may not equate with that of the shaman, since the former retains the flow and infusion of subterranean energy that manifests in emotion, sensitization and responsiveness to changing conditions and circumstances. Again, there is no aim to disassociate body and consciousness in Fitzmaurice Voicework. There may be clarity and calm ultimately in communication, but the fertile chaotic substratum in all its humanity and complexity is still tangible.

Finally, Kalweit does qualify what is acceptable for a productive shamanic trance: Trance means healing through inner recuperation from the unending stream of external stimuli, from complex thinking, from complicated emotions. The trance, however, does not exclude all stimuli. On the contrary, it heightens perception and brings out the colorfulness and vividness and wonder of existence. But this occurs only after a phase of narrowing consciousness, which is what is defined as trance in the most restricted sense of the word (91).

Both the shaman and the Fitzmaurice trained actor are heading toward heightened perception, but in Fitzmaurice Voicework, the process is inclusive rather than exclusive with "inner recuperation" embracing complexity in thought, emotion and body sensations in order to heal. Freedom comes in choices made in willful surrender as well as willful confrontation, and heightened perception is pervasive not only at the point of narrowing focus but also in the throes of chaos. In addition, dovetailing off the parallel to falling, it is significant to acknowledge that in the Voicework, the actor has already fallen, because the tremor positions involve an actor in postures on the ground where investigation is not about the act of falling but the reaction to being grounded. Post fall scenarios are evoked, and from here the actor can strategize on methods of recovery and ascent.

STRUCTURING

Restructuring is about very precise thinking. While destructuring involves survival breathing, restructuring demands intentional breathing where the energy that creates the rhythm of breath is the fluctuation of thought toward speech choices. With restructuring, the actor moves from chaos to choice, and the transition is significantly informed by the understanding that what is being structured is the chaos encountered in destructuring. Ideally this is a process that leads from the inside to the outside. From the psychological precinct, Keleman informs this transition when he writes, "Middle ground is the great creative soup originating social form from creative chaos. It is the central moment of turning points, the space where something has ended and something may form. In middle ground bodily process becomes the educator, and those who are able to listen to and learn from themselves can participate in their own restructuring from the inside" (81-2). From the scientific viewpoint, in observing natural pattern formations, Gleick remarked:

> When solidification proceeds from outside to inside, as in an ice tray, the boundary generally remains stable and smooth, its speed controlled by the ability of the walls to draw away the heat. But when a crystal solidifies outward from an initial seed – as a snow-flake does, grabbing water molecules while it falls through mois-ture-laden air – the process becomes unstable (309).

This instability is the quality that gives structuring its dynamic, live character. Structuring is a process rather than a fixed shape. While following a prescribed for-mula of muscle usage, those muscles are also subject to degree of structuring by the specificity of shifting thought. As Rudolf Arnheim states: "The structural theme must be conceived dynamically, as a pattern of forces, not an arrangement of static shapes" (33). The challenging transaction the actor must negotiate is balancing the influence of consciousness with spontaneity. The shift from the womb of chaos to the external world of communication and muscular expenditure can be hazardous to the fertility of imagination if the actor in transition becomes mechanical.

A distinction must be made between consciousness that supports creative energy and self-consciousness that inhibits it. The aim is to bring the clarity gained from chaos into a process of expression that ultimately become as reflexive as the habits and patterns it replaces, while keeping, in the spirit of growth, the possibility of gen-erating new forms for communication. This suggests an innate wisdom that chaos taps into, re-covers, and utilizes through sound and speech. Choice couples with spontaneity when the actor selects modalities of expression that honor the integrity of the chaotic inner world. Precisely, this involves making selections of breathing and sounding that do not violate the actor's instrument through squeezing, straining or gripping. Intention is positive tension that supports impulses rather than restrains them. Just as tremoring leads to structure, structure craves chaos to stay vital. A metaphor can be seen in nature when Briggs notes that, " Once formed, the self-organized structure stays 'alive' by drawing nourishment from the surrounding flux and disorder. This is what happens when tornados and other cyclonic winds form out of turbulence. To keep themselves going, they feed off of the thunderstorms, moisture, steep temperature and pressure gradients, and turbulence that gave them birth" (Fractals 112). This synergistic relationship is maintained in Fitzmaurice

Voicework through keeping structuring spontaneous, in regard to outer feedback with the environment, through focus-line in tandem with global breath and the flow of inner chaos while acting.

FOCUS AND PLAY

Fitzmaurice uses the term "focus-line" in assisting the actor bridging inner and outer realties. The focus-line introduces linear perspective into the non-linear domain of chaotic tremoring. In appreciating the idea of focus-line, one regards the creative balance between chaos and organization. Sheldrake points out that, "Chaos is never eliminated. There's always an indeterminism or spontaneity at all levels of organization" (26). If the speculation put forth by Walter J. Freeman is accurate, "... that chaos underlies the ability of the brain to respond flexibly to the outside world and to generate novel activity patterns, including those that are experienced as fresh ideas" (78), then interpersonal communication also involves chaos. The chaotic underpinning in both inner and outer worlds may provide a more fluid transition or continuum between them. In Fitzmaurice Voicework, rather than experienced as cessation, chaos is extended and structured on a line of focus. Structured breathing with a maintained perspectival focus- line creates a metaphoric tightrope upon which communion is expressed, both via an actor's need to perform an action and informed by reception from inner and outer worlds. The balancing act of the performer is a blend of disruptive chaos and willfully organized intention. The act of communion involves two relationships that occur between the actor and the self, juxtaposed with the actor and the other.

According to Ralph Abraham, "The mind somehow follows the eye and extends itself so as to actually engulf the object being viewed, to know it through intimate touch. Cognition is then a kind of engulfing, like eating" (Sheldrake, McKenna, and Abraham 79). Fitzmaurice points out that this sensuous seeing is layered by the shar-ing of air and vocal vibrations to create a field of play between actors ("The Actor's Voice Interview" 10). Coming full circle to the paradox of chaos theory, Briggs and Peat extend the term meaning self-renewal–*autopoesis*–to include interplay with the environment:

> Autopoietic systems are remarkable creatures of paradox. For example, because autopoietic structures are self-renewing, they are highly autonomous, each one having its separate identity, which

it continuously maintains. Yet, like other open systems autopoietic structures are also inextricably embedded in and inextricably merged with their environment – which is necessarily a far –from equilibrium environment of high energy flows involving food, sunlight, available chemicals and heat…Autopoietic structures have definite boundaries, such as a semipermeable membrane, but the boundaries are open and connect the system with almost unimaginable complexity to the world around it" (Mirror 154).

Survival breathing transitions into structured breathing in Fitzmaurice Voicework. In tremoring, survival breathing is elicited through arousing the autonomic nervous system. Survival strategies involve adaptations to inner and outer environment. Self-renewal is achieved in these adaptations by incorporating information coming in from those environments. Fitzmaurice Voicework taps into this autopoietic process through a voice that reflects self-renewing transactions between the myriad flexibility of tremoring with the autonomous stability of focus and centering. Structure comes about through the interplay of needs to adapt to dynamic shifting inner and outer environments. Conversation plays with conversion as the actor emerges from the destructured world. The skills obtained in destructuring, involving developing sensitivity to changing inner terrain, apply as the actor re-experiences outer reality in dialogue with another actor. The lesson learned from destructuring is that change must flow to release tensions and unearth insights. The paradigm shift from bracing to embracing flow and change allows for a vibrant feedback loop in communicating actors.

Play figures prominently in Fitzmaurice Voicework. Often, after the arduous confrontations engendered by dismantling tensions in destructuring, one discovers that effort converts instantly into play. The aim in Fitzmaurice Voicework is to play true, as distinguished by Bohm and Peat from the false play of illusion, delusion and collusion (48). The Voicework, in this respect, is a process that brings the actor to points of bifurcation where choice and consciousness come into play, where chaos plays the role of the trickster in altering linear perceptions to fractal ones and where the actor is given more texture and complexity to make what Fitzmaurice calls "brilliant selection" ("The Actor's Voice" 4). Fitzmaurice Voicework, developed non-theoretically, but purely through physical play and experimentation, is chaos in process and action.

CHAPTER FIVE:
CONCLUSION: WEAVING OUT OF CHAOS

It is important to point out that Fitzmaurice Voicework does not leave the performer in a state of chaos. Ultimately, the actor must weave the various threads informing and forming the organization of the Voicework, such as bioenergetics, yoga, shiatsu, subtle body anatomy, and western vocal technique, into the text. It is the actor's reification of the textual fabric that is the capstone of Fitzmaurice Voicework. This significant transition turns its therapeutic underpinnings toward artistic endeavor. Bioenergetics, yoga and shiatsu's contributions enlarge the density and vocabulary of the Voicework, giving more in-roads to the performer's liberation. They are all systems of transformation and recovery requiring inner listening as well as fluid expression. But while Fitzmaurice Voicework shares a common goal with these disciplines in removing muscular and mental blocks that inhibit the freedom of life flow, it makes a distinction in directing that flow toward the creative, communicative demands of theater, film and television. This work acknowledges a therapeutic essence without becoming limited or bogged down by it. The Voicework is more growth oriented than illness oriented, and yet by claiming growth orientation, there is an implicit inclusion of disease resolution. Fitzmaurice Voicework is potent therapy that can make significant changes in how a person organizes physical, mental, emotional and spiritual energy. But the therapeutic benefits always occur in the context and service of theatrical demands and are by-products rather than ends in themselves. Unlike many confrontational approaches to acting and voice, Fitzmaurice Voicework maintains a humble attitude toward the sanctity and integrity of the individual actor and never violates the personal trust by aggressively probing into the private life. On the other hand, the actor is given space to explore personal demons if elicited in conjunction with the destructuring program. In that case, the actor is usually taking the initiative in determining the nature of the exploration and in setting the boundaries. But still the project that the Voicework shares with yoga is one of synthesis, and that is where the significance of the text comes into play. For it is here, in the text, that the actor is given the tools to manage the flow of destructured energy, and without that opportunity, the creative journey would be incomplete.

Another distinguishing factor of the Voicework is it openly admits to the sexual nature of sound vibration and release. This is in line with Darwin's theory concerning the sexual origin of the vocal apparatus when he noted, "…I have elsewhere attempted to show that these organs were first developed for sexual purposes, in order that one sex might call or charm the other" (354). While primed by bioenergetics and tantra, the Voicework always moves vocal discharge toward genuine union with theatrical partners, whether other actors or the audience. The infusion of sexual energy with sound in this context offers a full-bodied communication full of passion and creative juice. The importance of embodying the voice, not only in identifying those muscles and organs usually associated with speech, but through the totality of physical release, availability and freedom in tremoring, gives more potential for textured, authentic expression. The transportation of global breath through the global body further extends and transmits sound through the theatrical realm. This internal/external union is achieved through the yoga of Fitzmaurice Voicework as part of its reconciliatory project. The Voicework interfaces yoga with bioenergetics in the practical reconciliation called for by Alexander Lowen. The connecting link is the breath, and Fitzmaurice as the yogi, Joel Kramer, seeks a blend of sensuality and spirituality through this agency. Her exercises are grounded in the body but allow discourse with the actor's spirit through contacting, via inspiration, the deep sources of communicative needs and charging them with the full infusion of the higher centers of consciousness. Thus, the actor is endowed with passion and intelligence that fluidly exchange one into the other. Tremoring, as a form of meditation in motion, does not seek to transcend in the theological sense as much as integrate, transmute, sublimate and transform creative potency via breath into positive expression. In the final analysis, the Voicework manifests spirituality through action and doing.

Fitzmaurice does address the practical business of theater, such as the standards debate as well. Language and standards live through their fluidity, since they are subject to change, and this is reflected in the Voicework's expansive view of phonetics, dialects and speech. Like the language it assists the actor in expressing, Fitzmaurice Voicework avoids calcification through maintaining a dynamic laterality with all brands of speech. In this way, no particular mode of pronunciation is elevated to the apex of a hierarchy. All acquisition and shaping of speech sounds occurs instead in the democratic spirit of heterarchy and only move into a preferred choice in relation to the specifics of the character created. Chaos theory instructs the Voicework in this open-ended porosity to prepare the actor with a multiplicity of sound choices that organize into ordered patterns of speech through sensitized response to character, text and the particulars of the theatrical milieu.

The density of the work is attributed to its ongoing dialogue with such debates, its functional interface with diverse Western and Eastern disciplines, and its inclusion of textual analysis and rhetorical figures. The Voicework both sustains tradition and welcomes innovation, for density is matched by porosity. While having a guiding set of foundational principles, it is the porosity of the Voicework that allows it to thrive in a constant state of discourse with itself and with other systems that are growth oriented. In this way, the student is invited to blossom in unique individuality. The goal is never to produce clone-like actors who all sound the same. It is understood that true liberation does not equate with enslavement to a technique, and the Voicework tools are provided not to impose a prescribed set of codifications on the actor but to unearth the full individual vocal potential. The actor is empowered to discover and carve out a totally personalized path to creative expression. Similarly, the spirit of fostering and nurturing individuals appears in Fitzmaurice's summons to the teachers that she trains. Fitzmaurice is not interested in sending out exact replicas of herself into the world. There is, of course, a fundamental demand to understand and master the deep theory that undergirds the work and gives it its integrity, but she encourages each teacher to explore and develop specific talents in relationship to the work. She welcomes experimentation. Fitzmaurice trained teachers bring a wide variety of backgrounds to the work including, singing, movement, dance, psychotherapy, speech pathology, alternative medicine, public speaking as well as expertise in systems of body alignment, acting, text, speech and dialects. The Voicework offers a common ground of dialogue between these artist/practitioners through the essential destructuring/restructuring motif.

The vibrancy of this work is that it is an open system and demands that it's community of practitioners–teachers as well as students–continue to explore the gaps in our knowledge about how the voice works and how to more effectively communicate. It is never a system of closure, and this insures its durability. What gives Fitzmaurice Voicework its currency and longevity is not just the lively East/West dialogue that resonates within the approach but its practical viability and application. In the same way that the Voicework demands an emergence from chaos, it also stretches from esoteric and therapeutic roots toward a very mundane usage in the real world. The vastness of the dialogue is so expansive that it may include a variety of practitioners and as such constitutes the restoration of a unity between oration, singing and acting. But just as chaos theory is not pointing the way back to a reoccurrence of a primeval chaotic world, the Voicework is not looking to reproduce the methods of the 19th century. The viability of Fitzmaurice Voicework is its interrogation of the past via destructuring in order to restructure energy in completely innovative ways in the present. It is in the here and now that the Voicework offers the possibility for reconciliation, unity and synthesis for clearer, passionate and life-altering communication. While Catherine Fitzmaurice has been carrying out this research for the past three decades, her pioneering work furnishes an open field for further exploration in the exciting study of the human voice.

WORKS CITED

Ajaya, Swami. <u>Psychotherapy East and West</u>. 1983. Honesdale, Pennsylvania: The Himalayan International Institute of Yoga Science and Philosophy of the U.S.A., 1997.

—. <u>Yoga Psychology</u>. 2nd ed. Glenview, Illinois: Himalayan International Institute of Yoga Science and Philosophy, 1976.

Anderson, Virgil A. <u>Training the Speaking Voice</u>. 2nd ed. New York: Oxford UP, 1961.

Arnheim, Rudolf. <u>Entropy and Art:An Essay on Disorder and Order</u>. Berkeley, California: University of California Press, 1971.

Avalon, Arthur [Sir John Woodroffe] . <u>The Serpent Power</u>. London: Luzac & Co, 1919. New York: Dover, 1974.

Baker, Elsworth. <u>Man in the Trap</u>. Princeton, New Jersey: The American College of Orgonomy Press, 2000.

Bandler, Richard, and John Grinder. <u>Frogs Into Princes</u>. Moab, Utah: Real People Press, 1979.

Berry, Cicely. "That Secret Voice." <u>The Vocal Vision</u>. Eds. Marion Hampton and Barbara Acker. New York: Applause Books, 1997. 25-35.

—. <u>The Actor and the Text</u>. New York: Applause Theatre Books, 1997.

—. <u>Voice and the Actor</u>. London: George C. Harrap & Co., 1973.

Berry, Michael. <u>Exploring Chaos</u>. Ed. Nina Hall. New York: W. W. Norton & Co. 1994.

Briggs, John. <u>Fractals: The Patterns of Chaos</u>. New York: Simon and Schuster, 1992.

Bohm, David. <u>Wholeness and the Implicate Order</u>. 1980. New York: Routledge Classics, 2002.

Bohm, David, and David Peat. <u>Science, Order and Creativity</u>. 2nd ed. London: Routledge, 2000.

Brennan, Barbara Ann. Hands of Light: <u>A Guide to Healing through the Human Energy Field</u>. New York: Bantam, 1988.

Briggs, John, and David Peat. Seven Life Lessons of Chaos. New York: Harper Perennial, 2000.

—. Turbulent Mirror. New York: Harper & Row, 1990.

Campbell, Joseph. The Hero With a Thousand Faces. 1949. Princeton: Princeton UP, 1973.

Capra, Fritjof. The Tao of Physics. 4th ed. Boston: Shambhala Publications, 2000.

Chekhov, Michael. To the Actor. New York: Harper and Row, 1953.

Colaianni, Louis. The Joy of Phonetics and Accents. Kansas City: Joy Press, 1994.

Cole, Toby, and Helen Krich Chinoy, eds. Actors on Acting. 1949. New York: Three River Press, 1970.

Conger, John. Jung & Reich: The Body as Shadow. 1988. Berkeley, California: North Atlantic Books, 2005.

Corrigan, Mary. "Psycho-Physical Techniques and Their Relevance to Voice and Actor Training." The Vocal Vision. Eds. Marion Hampton and Barbara Acker. New York: Applause Books, 1997. 93-105.

Court, Penelope. "The Effect of Humanistic Psychology on Voice Training for the Actor." Thesis. Goodman School of Drama of the Art Institute of Chicago, 1978.

Darwin, Charles. The Expression of the Emotions in Man and Animals. 1965. Chicago: The University of Chicago Press, 1974.

Deren, Maya. The Divine Horsemen: The Living Gods of Haiti. 1953. Kingston, New York: McPherson & Company, 2004.

Desikachar, T.K.V. The Heart of Yoga. Rochester, Vermont: Inner Traditions International, 1999.

Diderot, Denis. The Paradox of Acting. New York: Hill and Wang, 1957.

Drury, Neville. The Healing Power: A Handbook of Alternative Medicine and Natural Health. London, Frederick Muller Ltd., 1981.

Eliade, Mircea. Shamanism: Archaic Techniques of Ecstasy. 1964. Princeton: Princeton UP, 1974.

Feuerstein, Georg. The Yoga Tradition. Prescott, Arizona: Home Press, 2001.

Fitzmaurice, Catherine. "Breathing is Meaning." The Vocal Vision. Eds. Marion Hampton and Barbara Acker. New York: Applause Books, 1997. 247-252.

—. "The Actor's Voice: Interview with Catherine Fitzmaurice." Acting Now. Interview by Eugene Douglass. Issue 2. www.actingnow.com, 2004.

—. "Structured Breathing." VASTA Newsletter. Vol. 17, Number 1, Spring 2003.

—. "Zeami Breathing." <u>Standard Speech and Other Contemporary issues in Professional Voice and Speech Training</u>. Ed. Rocco Dal Vera. Voice and Speech Trainers Vol. 1, Association, Inc., Number 1, 2000. 195-202.

—. Personal Interviews. 23 Feb. 2005, 27 Sept. 2005, 9 Oct. 2005, 12 Nov. 2005, 10 Jan. 2006.

Floyd, Keith. "Of Time and the Mind." <u>Fields Within Fields Within Fields</u>. Number 10 (1973-4) : 47-57.

Frawley, David. <u>Tantric Yoga</u>. 2nd ed. Twin Lakes, WI: Lotus Press, 2003.

Freeman, Richard. <u>The Yoga Matrix: The Body As a Gateway to Freedom</u>. Audio CD # 1, track 11. Boulder, CO: Sounds True, 2003.

Freeman, Walter J. "The Physiology of Perception." <u>Scientific American</u>. Vol.264 Number 2 (Feb. 1991) : 78-85.

Funderburk, James. <u>Science Studies Yoga</u>. Honesdale, PA: Himalayan International Institute of Yoga Science & Philosophy, 1977.

Gleick, James. <u>Chaos: Making a New Science</u>. New York: Penguin, 1987.

Goldberger, Ary L., David R. Rigney, and Bruce J. West. "Chaos and Fractals in Human Physiology." <u>Scientific American</u>. Vol.262. Number 2 (Feb.1990) : 42-49.

Goodman, Saul. <u>The Book of Shiatsu</u>. Garden City Park, New York: Avery, 1990.

Grossinger, Richard. <u>Planet Medicine: Origins</u>. 2 vols. Berkeley, CA: North Atlantic Books, 1995.

Higgins, Mary, and Chester M. Raphael, Eds. <u>Reich Speaks of Freud</u>. New York: Farrar, Straus and Giroux, 1967.

Iyengar, B.K.S. <u>Light on Pranayama</u>. New York: Crossroads, 2003.

—. <u>Light on Yoga</u>. 1966. New York: Schochen, 1979.

Jaynes, Julian. <u>The Origin of Consciousness in the Breakdown of the Bicameral Mind</u>. Boston: Houghton Mifflin Company, 1976.

Jones, Daniel. <u>English Pronouncing Dictionary</u>. 1917. Eds. Peter Roach and James Hartman. 15th ed. Cambridge: Cambridge UP, 1997.

Jung, C. G. <u>Psychology and Alchemy</u>. 8th printing Rev. ed. Princeton: Princeton UP, 1993.

Kalweit, Holger. <u>Shamans, Healers and Medicine Men</u>. Trans. Michael H. Kohn. Boston: Shambhala Publications, 1992.

Keleman, Stanley. <u>Somatic Reality</u>. Berkeley, CA: Center Press, 1979.

Keller, Doug. "Reconcilable Differences." <u>Yoga Journal</u> Nov-Dec. 1999: 104-5.

Kellert, Stephen. In the Wake of Chaos. Chicago: University of Chicago Press, 1993.

Kenyon, John S., and Thomas A. Knott. A Pronouncing Dictionary of American English. Springfield, MA: Merriam-Webster, 1953.

Knight, Dudley. "Standard Speech: The Ongoing Debate." Standard Speech and Other Contemporary Issues in Professional Voice and Speech Training. Ed. Rocco Dal Vera. Voice and Speech Trainers Association, Inc., 2000. 31-54.

Kotzubei, Saul. Personal Interview. 30 Oct. 2005.

Kraftsow, Gary. Yoga for Transformation. New York: Penguin Compass, 2002.

—. Yoga For Wellness. New York: Penguin Compass, 1999.

Kramer, Joel. "Mind in Asana." Interview with Jeanne Malmgren Cameron. Yoga Journal Jul-Aug. 1986: 20-2.

—. "Yoga As Self-Transformation." Yoga Journal May-June. 1980: 1-10.

Krishnamurti, J. Freedom From the Known. New York: Harper Collins, 1969.

Lessac, Arthur. "From Beyond Wildness to Body Wisdom Vocal Life, and Healthful Functioning." The Vocal Vision. Eds. Marion Hampton and Barbara Acker. New York: Applause Books, 1997. 13-24.

—. The Use and Training of the Human Voice. 1960. Mountain View, CA: Mayfield Publishing Co.,1997.

Linklater, Kristin. Freeing Shakespeare's Voice. New York: Theatre Communications Group, 1992.

—. Freeing the Natural Voice. New York: Drama Book Publishers, 1976.

—. "Thoughts on Theatre, Therapy and the Art of Voice." The Vocal Vision. Eds. Marion Hampton and Barbara Acker. New York: Applause Books, 1997. 3-12.

Lorenz, Edward N. The Essence of Chaos. 1993. Seattle: University of Washington Press, 1995.

Lowen, Alexander. Bioenergetics. 1975. New York: Penguin Compass, 1976.

—. Pleasure. 1970. New York: Penguin, 1982.

—. The Betrayal of the Body. 1967. New York: Collier Books, 1971.

—. The Language of the Body. 1958. New York: Collier Books, 1971.

—. The Way to Vibrant Health. New York: Harper and Row, 1977.

Mandelbrot, Benoit. Exploring Chaos. Ed. Nina Hall. New York: W. W. Norton & Co. 1994.

Martin, Jacqueline. Voice in the Modern Theatre. New York: Routledge, Chapman & Hall, Inc., 1991.

McLean, Margaret. Good American Speech. 1928. New York: E. P. Dutton, 1968.

McTeague, James H. Before Stanislavsky: American Professional Acting Schools and Acting Theory 1875-1925. Metuchen, New Jersey: The Scarecrow Press, Inc., 1993.

Melton, Joan and Kenneth Tom. One Voice: Integrating Singing Technique and Theatre Voice Training. Portsmouth, New Hampshire: Heinemann, 2003.

Mitchell, Stephen. Tao Te Ching. New York: Harper & Row, 1988.

Moses, Paul J. The Voice of Neurosis. New York: Grune & Stratton, 1954.

Muldoon, Sylvan and Hereward Carrington. The Projection of the Astral Body. Boston, MA: Weiser Books, 1969.

Peat, David. Synchronicity. New York: Bantam Books, 1988.

Peak, David, and Michael Frame. Chaos Under Control: The Art and Science of Complexity. New York: W. H. Freeman and Company, 1994.

Percival, Ian. Exploring Chaos. Ed. Nina Hall. New York: W. W. Norton & Co. 1994.

Pierrakos, John C. Core Energetics. 1987. Mendocino, CA: LifeRhythm Publication, 1990.

Price, Cecil. Theatre in the Age of Garrick. Totowa, New Jersey: Rowman and Littlefield, 1973.

Prigogine, Ilya, and Isabelle Stengers. Order Out of Chaos. New York: Bantam Books, 1984.

Rama, Swami, Rudolph Ballentine, and Swami Ajaya. Yoga and Psychotherapy. 1976.

Honesdale, PA: The Himalayan International Institute of Yoga Science and Philosophy, 1981.

Rama, Swami, Rudolph Ballentine, and Alan Hymes. Science of Breath.1979. Honesdale, PA: The Himalayan International Institute of Yoga Science and Philosophy, 1981.

Raphael, Bonnie. "A Consumer's Guide to Voice and Speech Training." The Vocal Vision. Eds. Marian Hampton and Barbara Acker. New York: Applause Books, 1997. 203-213.

Reich, Wilhelm. Character Analysis. Trans. Vincent R. Carfagno. 1945. New York: Simon and Schuster, 1972.

—. Cosmic Superimposition. Trans. Therese Pol. 1951. New York: Farrar, Straus and Giroux, 1973.

—. Ether, God and Devil. Trans. Therese Pol. 1949. New York: Farrar, Straus and Giroux, 1973.

—. The Function of the Orgasm. Trans. Vincent R. Carfagno. 1942. New York: Farrar, Straus and Giroux, 1973.

—. The Mass Psychology of Fascism. 1946. New York: Farrar, Straus and Giroux, 1970.

—. The Sexual Revolution. Trans. Theodore P. Wolfe. 1945. New York: Farrar, Straus and Giroux, 1969.

Roach, Joseph R. The Player's Passion. 1993. Ann Arbor: The University of Michigan Press, 2002.

Rodenburg, Patsy. "Re-Discovering Lost Voices." The Vocal Vision Eds. Marian Hampton and Barbara Acker. New York: Applause Books, 1997. 37-41.

—. The Need for Words. 1993. London: Methuen Drama, 1994.

—. The Right to Speak. New York: Routledge, 1992.

Ruelle, David. Chance and Chaos. Princeton: Princeton UP, 1993.

Saint-Denis, Michel. Training for the Theatre. New York: Theatre Arts Books, 1982.

Schiffmann, Erich. Yoga: The Spirit and Practice of Moving Into Stillness. New York: Pocket Books, 1996.

Schultz, Barbara L. "New Age Shiatsu." The Holistic Health Handbook. Bauman, et al., Eds. Berkeley, CA: And/Or Press, 1978.

Sheldrake, Rupert, Terrance McKenna and Ralph Abraham. 1992. Chaos, Creativity, and Cosmic Consciousness. Rochester, Vermont: Park Street Press, 2001.

Skinner, Edith. Speak With Distinction. New York: Applause Books, 1990.

Solomon, Philip, et al., eds. Sensory Deprivation. Cambridge, MA: Harvard UP, 1961.

Stanislavski, Constantin. An Actor Prepares. Trans. Elizabeth Reynolds Hapgood. 1936. New York: Theatre Arts Books, 1970.

—. Building a Character. Trans. Elizabeth Reynolds Hapgood. 1949. New York: Theatre Arts Books, 1969.

Stewart, Ian. Does God Play Dice?. 1989. Malden, MA: Blackwell Publishing, 2002.

Svoboda, Robert, and Arnie Lade. Tao and Dharma. 1995. Twin Lakes, WI: Lotus Press, 2005.

Talbot, Michael. <u>Mysticism and the New Physics</u>. New York: Penguin Arkana, 1993.

Todd, Mabel Elsworth. <u>The Thinking Body</u>. 1937. New York: Dance Horizons, 1959.

Turner, Clifford. <u>Voice and Speech in the Theatre</u>. 1950. London: Sir Isaac Pitman & Sons,1966.

Vishnudevananda, Swami. <u>The Complete Illustrated Book of Yoga</u>. 1960. New York: Julian Press, 1961.

<u>Webster's New World Dictionary and Thesaurus</u>. CD-Rom. Macmillian Digital Publishing Co, 1997.

Wilson, Garff B. <u>A History of American Acting</u>. Bloomington, Indiana: Indiana UP, 1966.

Withers-Wilson, Nan. <u>Vocal Direction for the Theatre</u>. New York: Drama Book Publishers, 1993.

Xinnong, Cheng, et al., eds. <u>Chinese Acupuncture and Moxibustion</u>. Beijing: Foreign Language Press, 1987.

Printed in the USA
CPSIA information can be obtained
at www.ICGtesting.com
LVHW011546291123
765067LV00004B/443